Dear Nancy & Tomas,

I'm so blessed for our special f... all these years. I ... wonderful to see you ... in "Minnesnowda", eh! :) I hope you are inspired ... my journey of redemption. In Yeshua's amazing love,

Goldie :) ♡

Ephesians 3:20!
Psalm 122:6!

Jane Winn is one of the most irrepressibly joyful and positive persons I have ever known. The trials of her early life would have destroyed almost anyone, but she is not merely a survivor. She is an *overcomer*. She has learned to see the beauty of rainbows in the night, and her faith and enthusiasm are contagious. I highly recommend this book. Just be prepared to weep and wonder.

Joan E. Boydell, MA, LPC
Former Executive Director of Amnion Pregnancy Center
Center Services Specialist, Care Net

I have known Jane "Goldie" Winn since 1987, and her gift of joy is contagious. She has a gift of encouragement and knows how to minister to the deep hurts of her clients as a professional counselor in a variety of settings. This book highlights her deep passion for the Lord and very unique life experiences, and I am excited to highly recommend it. Hers is truly a story of redemption!

Dr. Rhona Epstein, Psy.D
Certified Addictions Counselor
Author of *Food Triggers* and
Satisfied: A 90 Day Spiritual Journey Toward Food Freedom

With great courage and vulnerability, Goldie has opened her heart to us, and given us a glimpse into the powerful working of the Lord in her life. As her captivating story unfolds, we will witness the way the Lord has transformed the trials of her life into beauty and given the pain of her life meaning. We will watch her walk forth in victory, fulfilling the purpose God has assigned her, as she brings His healing touch to those who are hurting.

Celeste Li, M.D.
Medical Director, First Care Women's Clinic
Author of *Triumph Over Suffering*

RAINBOW IN THE NIGHT

A Journey of Redemption

JANE "GOLDIE" WINN, MSS

Plum
Tree
Ministries

I would like to be remembered as someone who encouraged many, believed the best before the worst, and sprinkled joy wherever she went!

Plum Tree Ministries

Jupiter, Florida
plumtreeministries@gmail.com
"The surviving remnant of the house of Judah will again take root downward and bear fruit upward." Isaiah 37:31

Rainbow in the Night
A Journey of Redemption
Copyright © 2019 by Jane Goldie Winn

Plum Tree Ministries
210 Jupiter Lakes Blvd., #5105, Jupiter, FL 33458 USA

ISBN-13: 978-0-9993393-0-5
Printed in United States of America

Cover painting by Sherry Heller at biblicalsculpture.com
Cover photography by Sharleen Stuart at sharleenstuart.com
Design and layout by Anna M. Pizzoferrato - i.a.m.pizzoferrato@gmail.com

Some names and identifying details of people in this book have been changed to protect the privacy of those individuals.

Contents

Foreword   ix

Introduction   xi

Chapter 1: A Bruised Reed   1

Chapter 2: Chasing After the Wind   17

Chapter 3: Reclaiming Lost Ground   31

Chapter 4: A New Creation!   41

Chapter 5: Marrying My Soul Mate   53

Chapter 6: Trusting an Unknown Future to a Known God   63

Chapter 7: My Hope is Lost   73

Chapter 8: Restoration of Joy   85

Chapter 9: My Hidden Treasure   93

Chapter 10: Rivers in the Desert   99

Chapter 11: The Lord Takes Delight in Me   105

Chapter 12: Forgiveness is a Process, Not an Event   111

Chapter 13: Restorative Love   117

Chapter 14: Delight in My Lord   123

Chapter 15: You Will Be a Mother to Many   129

Chapter 16: The Gift of Family   137

Chapter 17: The Stage is Set   143

Chapter 18: A Leap of Faith   151

Chapter 19: Earthly Paradise   155

Chapter 20: Test of Faith   159

Chapter 21: Abiding in His Presence   165

Chapter 22: Embracing My Calling   169

Chapter 23: Freedom is a Choice   173

Chapter 24: Nothing is Impossible With God   181

Resources   191

Acknowledgments   193

About the Author   197

Foreword

*O*ne night a number of years ago, as I was driving in England with my oldest son, we saw an actual rainbow in the night stretching across the black sky. It was a sign of hope and a testament that nothing is impossible to our awesome God!

This lovely book by Goldie, this special opening of her heart, is also a testament of God's grace, for He brought her out of darkness into the light of His love. Just as that rainbow transformed the darkness, God's love beautifully transformed her life.

As you take this journey with her, you can't help but be amazed at the patience and the wisdom and the tender love of the Lord as evidenced in the changes He wrought in her life. He lifted her from a place of darkness and depression and longing for love, and gave her the gift of joy.

May the Lord bless you as you read the pages of this book.

Esther Korson
Author of *I Am My Beloved's*
and *The Voice of My Beloved: A Handbook on Obedience*
estherkorson.com

Introduction

*A*lthough a rainbow in the night sounds impossible, maybe even mythical, these striking "moonbows" are indeed a real but rare phenomenon. Just like solar rainbows, lunar rainbows are formed by the refraction of light in many water droplets, but the light source for a lunar rainbow is moonlight rather than sunlight.[1]

Because the light reflecting off the moon is much less intense than the light of the sun, it is difficult for the human eye to detect the colors in a lunar rainbow. To the human eye, a rainbow in the night may appear grey or white. However, all the colors are indeed present, and do become visible in long-exposure photographs.[2]

In many ways, my life parallels a rainbow in the night. At times I felt dark, devoid of color and meaning, but all along every bright and beautiful hue was visible to my Creator. Just like the radiant colors of a moonbow are revealed by a long-exposure photograph, after decades of walking with the Lord, vivid shades are emerging from my darkness. Over the years, the Lord has made visible to me the luminous colors of my life, colors that had been previously veiled from my sight. Now, as the Lord has granted me deeper and deeper healing, and opened my eyes to the brilliance of His work in my life, I have come to appreciate the fulfillment of this promise from Isaiah,

> *"I will give you hidden treasures,*
> *riches stored in secret places,*
> *so that you may know that I am the LORD,*
> *the God of Israel, who summons you by name."*
> Isaiah 45:3

I realize that I will not see the fullness of these colors until I can see this rainbow more clearly from an eternal perspective. But in the meantime, I'd like to share what the Lord has shown me as I can perceive it from my finite perspective.

My story is a journey of *redemption*. Redemption involves setting a captive free through the payment of a ransom price. I have indeed been set free from darkness and depression and futility by the death and resurrection of Jesus, *Yeshua* in Hebrew. Yet in the Lord's hands, redemption is far more than a release. Redemption is a seemingly unbelievable exchange: I give the Lord my sin and shame and failures, and He gives me not only forgiveness and eternal life, but beauty from my ashes. Somehow, in a way I cannot even begin to fathom, He miraculously brings treasures and purpose out of my failures. Not *despite* my failures, but *out of* my failures.

I invite you to join me on my journey. You may want to bring a notebook and a pen so you can journal your answers to the questions at the end of each chapter. And, as we travel these pages together, I pray that my story will enable you to focus on the God of the bigger picture, the God who is always working, the God who transforms failures into beauty. My hope is that you will indeed begin to see the colors emerging in your own life, colors that burst out of the hidden treasures. I pray that you, too, will be able to look back and say with certainty,

"And we know that God causes all things to work together for good to those who love God, to those who are called according to His purpose." Romans 8:28 NASB

------

[1]Richard Whitaker, et al., *Weather Watching*, San Francisco, CA, Fog City Press, 2006, p 272-273.

[2] astronomytrek.com/examining-the-phenomenon-of-lunar-rainbows, accessed 6/10/19.

Chapter 1
A Bruised Reed

"A bruised reed He will not break
And a dimly burning wick He will not extinguish;
He will faithfully bring forth justice."

Isaiah 42:3 NASB

I vividly remember my early childhood home. We lived in a sprawling English Tudor home up on a hill overlooking the Connecticut River in Holyoke, Massachusetts. The house was every kid's dream. There were secret passageways, a huge wrap-around porch, beautiful foliage, and spacious rooms with French doors. My father was early in his practice as a physician, and I fondly remember his reciting the names of bones and muscles as we washed and dried dishes together. Those were rather carefree days.

My father's name was Selig Morley Korson. His family came to this country from the Ukraine, settling as new immigrants in one of the teeming neighborhoods in Brooklyn, New York. His parents were observant Jews, and although I never met his mother, I heard that she was a very strict disciplinarian. My grandfather Joseph was a laborer, painting houses to make a living. He was described as a gentle soul, very kind, compassionate, and unassuming. I am named after him; my Hebrew name is Josepha.

My father's dream was to pursue medicine. Times were difficult with five other siblings, and he took various jobs to work his way through medical school. In addition, one of his sisters, Ann, a registered nurse, helped him financially. My father was extremely bright and graduated valedictorian of his class.

During World War II, my father served as a physician in the medical corp. His experiences helping soldiers who were traumatized by the ravages of war compelled him to pursue psychiatry. A second impetus for this decision was born out of tragedy. Prior to the war, he had a thriving medical practice in Pennsylvania. When he went off to war, he had placed all of his medical equipment from his two offices in storage. When he returned home in 1945, he learned that his storage unit had been destroyed by fire. He had not purchased fire insurance, so everything was lost. He realized that a psychiatric practice would not require medical equipment.

My mother, Beatrice Goldman, grew up in an observant Jewish family in Hartford, Connecticut. Both her parents were gentle and warm people. She was the oldest of four girls, and because her father became ill while she was in high school, she never had the opportunity to attend college. She went to work to help support the rest of the family, and according to her sisters, she was the strong one.

My mother was a beautiful woman. She modeled at G. Fox & Company, an elegant department store in Hartford. As a matter of fact, she was one of the few models who could wear Scarlett O'Hara's dress with her eighteen-inch waistline! With her beautiful blue eyes and stunning long golden curly hair, she was often mistaken as a movie star.

My father and mother met at a resort in the Catskills. According to my mother, she had many suitors. However, when she met my father, although he was ten years older than she was, she intuitively knew that he needed her, so she decided to allow him to win her over. Once they married, the young couple faced many challenges. Perhaps the most challenging was Selig's mother, who attempted to come between them. My mother finally gave her husband

2

an ultimatum: choose her, or Mother. He made the decision to stand up to his mother, perhaps for the first time in his life.

Three girls were born into the Korson family. I am the middle child, born in 1949. My sister Esther is six years older and Cathy five years younger.

From the time that my older sister Esther was a little girl, my father hated her, picking on her and abusing her both physically and verbally. The constant rejection that Esther experienced is beyond words. Because my father abused my sister so severely, I developed a real fear of my father. I decided that I would be a "good girl", and would make sure that I pleased him. My fear and anger eventually resulted in depression, and most of my childhood I used to wish that either I or my father would die. It breaks my heart to realize that I took my anger out on my younger sister Cathy, which caused a rift in our relationship for many years.

As things began to worsen, I escaped into the world of books. *The Bobbsey Twins* and *Nancy Drew* became my safe and exciting "friends". I spent hours alone in my room, devouring every book I could get my hands on. I had such an active imagination that every character came alive.

In 1954, when I was five, my father was offered a position as an Assistant Superintendent at a Veterans Administration hospital in St. Petersburg, Florida. We left beautiful New England for warm and sunny Florida. We lived on Paradise Island and bought a lovely home on the bay. We often watched porpoises frolicking in the bay while eating dinner.

About three years after we moved to Florida, my father was offered a prestigious position in Independence, Iowa. He was asked to assume the post of Superintendent at a very large state mental health institute with 1100 patients and over 500 employees.

This was a major move, but to me it felt like an adventure. After all, who ever heard of Independence, Iowa? And we would live right on the hospital grounds! When we arrived, my first glimpse was of the main building, a formidable looking structure, built in 1873. There were bars on all the windows, and people dressed in white starched uniforms walking from one building to another. When we got out of the car, my father exclaimed; "What have I gotten myself into? Well, my first administrative decision will have to be the removal of all those ugly bars from the windows. This place feels inhumane, and that has got to change!"

My father was quite a visionary even long before deinstitutionalization took place, which is the emptying out of many large state hospitals. Under his administration, the hospital was transformed from a custodial care institution into one of the most comprehensive mental health treatment centers in the country. Because of his many accomplishments in the field of psychiatry, he was honored by inclusion in *Who's Who in America*.

During my father's tenure, he and some of his colleagues created a museum to display an array of some of the most archaic forms of treatment measures for the mentally ill. Included were lobotomy instruments, ice packs, and straitjackets. There were also some very large round rollers with long handles. My father explained that these were actually floor polishers, but that patients used them for "therapy", beating paraffin into wood to help them work out their stress and anger. To this day, this museum continues to be available to the public for educational purposes.

As one can well imagine, growing up in a state hospital made for quite an interesting childhood. In the hospital building where the patients lived, a large hall separated the men's ward on one side and the women's ward on the other. Our kitchen and dining area was right next to an unlocked women's ward. Oftentimes patients would get confused and end up in our kitchen!

The rest of our living quarters were in the superintendent's apartment, which was housed on the second floor of the administration building. The apartment itself was a grand place, with high ceilings and a lounge big enough to seat one hundred people. Every room had beautiful marble fireplaces and huge windows. There was a sunroom that overlooked the spacious and well-maintained grounds. My mother had a gift of interior decorating, and she transformed the quarters into a comfortable and magnificent showplace.

My father was described by his colleagues as "one of the last patriarchal superintendents". He knew many of the patients by name, and was very involved in the personal lives of his employees as well. Since many of the doctors on staff were from foreign countries, their own fathers often could not be present at their weddings. My father graciously stood in for those fathers.

Looking back at this time in my life, there were many valuable lessons I learned. I remember my father saying to us early on that even though these patients were mentally ill, they must be treated with dignity and care. He often reminded us, "But for the grace of God, there go I." This is where I learned tolerance and compassion, as I observed so many caring employees treating the patients with kindness and gentleness. One of my favorite memories, and probably what helped my father to earn his reputation as a patriarchal superintendent, was a concert for the psychiatric patients. It was held in the lounge area in our apartment. My father invited one hundred patients, and had hired a wonderful and gifted concert pianist, who was also the music therapist. Our housekeeping staff, as well as my mother, my two sisters and I, served tea sandwiches and coffee to the patients using our best silver. The look on their faces made this an incredibly memorable experience.

Before my father's tenure, there was a terrible stigma associated with mental illness. Many families were so ashamed that a family member had this affliction that often patients were dropped off at the hospital, never to see their families again. Sadly, some died and were even buried there. My father's work at the hospital significantly mitigated the stigma, but did not completely eliminate it. As superintendent, my father became, in a very real sense, a father to many of the patients that had little or no family contact.

A doctor who served under my father's administration for many years told me of a time when my father was called down to the employee cafeteria. This was before many of the psychotropic medicines had come onto the scene. On this particular day, a patient who had been working in the cafeteria suddenly flew into a rage, grabbed a huge butcher knife, leapt up onto a table, and began to threaten the employees in the room. When my father arrived, he asked every employee to leave the room so that he could be alone with the patient. He spoke so lovingly and gently to this patient that he came down from the table and handed my father the knife without a fight!

My father will always be remembered as "the Superintendent who enlightened the legislature". He was able to procure funding to provide a top-notch staff from around the world, and money to remodel some of the decrepit buildings on the grounds. Several buildings known as "the back wards" were demolished so that the hospital could be modernized. In 1969, a new children's unit was dedicated. The J.O. Cromwell Children's Unit is located on a sixteen-acre site south of the main building.

It is a modern, efficient, and comfortable setting for the children and adolescent patients in residence. To this day the Mental Health Institute of Independence, Iowa is one of the most renowned comprehensive treatment centers for the mentally challenged in America!

When my father arrived in 1958, this hospital functioned as a custodial care institution with over 1100 patients. By 1970, under my father's leadership, the hospital was fast becoming a short-term mental health facility, where patients were treated and equipped to re-enter society. The average daily census dropped from 1100 to 329 patients. Quite a contrast, to be sure!

Living in the main administration building in the hospital was like living in a fish bowl. The front doors of our apartment opened up to a beautiful and ornate staircase, which faced the spacious and beautiful grounds. The staircase emptied out into the entryway of the main building, leading into the lobby where the switchboard operator and my father's administrative suite of offices were located. Every time we left our apartment, we walked down this staircase. From the moment we opened our front doors, there were always patients and staff to greet. We always looked our best at all times since we had to keep up our image as the "first family" – or so it seemed.

Many years later, another member of the staff shared with me how the employees deeply respected my father. Whenever he would show up on a patient ward for the weekly rounds, the entire staff would rise to their feet as he walked into their presence. I'm told he never demanded that kind of respect, but the employees felt he earned it due to his compassionate and effective leadership.

Every Sunday night was movie night at the hospital. We had a huge auditorium with a balcony, and employees, their families, and patients were all invited. Every Thursday night we had a dance for the patients, with staff and patients providing live music. My father often joined the hospital band, since he played the saxophone and loved to entertain. I was learning the saxophone myself, and when I got older, I often joined the band too.

Holidays were another special treat for patients as well as employees and their families. The hospital was decorated beautifully, and people from the community, along with student nurses, put on variety shows and brought gifts for the patients, particularly at Christmas time. We were all treated to a delicious holiday dinner.

I have some very fond memories of those ten years that I lived in the hospital. My father had an excellent staff, and many of the doctors came from different countries. It was a unique opportunity to meet their children and learn about different cultures. My mother often held cooking classes, inviting the doctor's wives to take turns preparing meals from their particular countries. Afterwards, all the families would enjoy food from various parts of the world while dining in our apartment.

One day my mother had a very dramatic experience. She was having her morning coffee, when a female patient wandered into our kitchen by mistake. This particular patient was almost mute, and had been hospitalized for many years. Her husband was in a state penitentiary, and she had very little contact with her family. My mother described what followed as a serendipitous and miraculous event.

My mother began talking to this patient about a decision she made when we first arrived at the hospital. When we began moving into the Superintendent's apartment, my mother found some beautiful furniture that had been stored away, and she used that furniture to furnish our apartment. My mother went on to share that the furniture was made by inmates at that very state penitentiary where this patient's husband was serving his sentence. Well, at that moment, this woman, who had barely said a word for many years, began talking to my mother! She talked about her husband, her life, and her family. She was completely lucid. I'm sure my mother and this patient were both in a state of shock. Clearly something my mother had said unlocked a door in her mind that had been closed for many years. This woman was discharged not long after the event, and kept in touch with my mother for many years.

My father wanted the residents of Independence, Iowa to know how important the state hospital was to the economic well being of their town. We were all part of the same community, and my father wanted this town of about 5000 to become more aware of the hospital's contribution and to work closely with us. Many people resisted; they stayed away and continued to refer to the hospital as "that place on the hill". So my father decided to take matters into his own hands.

He had 500 employees. For one pay period, every employee was paid in $2.00 bills. Each employee was instructed to shop, buy groceries, and pay all of their bills using the $2.00 bills. This was a huge wake-up call for Independence, and from that moment on there was a new respect for the Mental Health Institute on the hill. This had such an impact on the town that a story was written and submitted to many newspapers across the country.

There were funny stories, too, and one I remember quite well happened late one night. At that time, we had one of the few alcoholic treatment centers in the country that was housed in a state hospital. Part of that center was locked, because some of the patients arrived in acute states and needed to be monitored until they could be moved to a more open unit. My father was always on call, and that memorable night he was summoned to the front of the hospital. Evidently, some of the patients who were attempting to escape had tied several rags together and were letting each other down from a window. The night watchman caught them and phoned my father, and their escape was thwarted.

This was a bittersweet time in my life, because the private persona of my father was incongruent with the public persona. He was so well respected by colleagues all over the world, presenting at world psychiatric conferences, publishing articles in several journals, and receiving the ultimate reward of an invitation to submit his bio for *Who's Who in America*. Inside our apartment, however, things were very different.

My father ran our family like a tight ship. Breakfast, lunch, and dinner were to be served exactly the same time each day. His anger towards my older sister Esther escalated. He would often tell my younger sister and me that he "hated Esther's guts", and that we should never grow up to be like her. My mother never openly dealt with my father's hatred of Esther. It wasn't until many years later, after my father's death, that with professional help my mother was finally able to face the reality that my father had not been a nice person. That helped her to heal emotionally and opened the door for my mother and Esther to become close friends.

However, when Esther was growing up, Mom was also very rejecting and treated Esther coldly. Altogether, it was an extremely frightening and confusing time for me. It was becoming increasingly difficult for me to bridge our public and private lives. I escaped deeper into the world of books, and turned my anger inward, since I was too afraid to confront my father. I became depressed, and my mother used to describe me as "that little girl with a pocket full of tears".

Esther was always a fighter and a dreamer, and somehow that gave her the strength to deal with her difficult life. Eventually, my father's older sister Sue came for a visit. Aunt Sue and some members of the hospital staff intervened when they could see that my father's rage towards Esther was out of control. They recommended that my parents send her to a boarding school in Wisconsin.

Esther had exhibited an unusual talent for the piano. When she was fourteen, after only six weeks of lessons, she had given a concert for the hospital staff, playing Beethoven, Steven Heller, and Chopin. Aunt Sue and the staff suggested to my parents that Esther could continue her piano studies at a boarding school. Although the boarding school they recommended was Catholic, it had an excellent reputation and an outstanding music program. My parents finally agreed with their recommendation, and at age fifteen, Esther left for Wisconsin.

Thankfully, Esther has an extremely high IQ, so school was never difficult for her. While she attended boarding school, one of the nuns, Sister Virgil, befriended Esther and showed her kindness and compassion. I believe the Lord used this nun to help her to feel loved by an adult, since love was not modeled very effectively by either of our parents. Esther graduated from high school at the age of 16 and completed a bachelor's degree in two years from a small Iowa university. Upon graduation from college, she was offered a full scholarship for a two year Master's Degree program in Social Work at the University of Connecticut. The scholarship was granted by the National Institute of Mental Health and included full tuition, as well as room and board.

It was at the University of Connecticut that she met Joe, a Catholic boy who was also pursuing a master's degree in social work. They courted and decided to marry. When

Esther told my father of her intentions, my father was livid. Marrying a non-Jewish person felt like a real betrayal to his faith, and he told her that she was "disowned". He forbade me, my mother, and my younger sister Cathy to have any contact with her, and declared that as far as he was concerned, she was dead. Whenever her name was mentioned, he would spit and walk out of the room.

This was a very difficult time in my life as well. I was in high school, and I was the only Jewish kid in the entire school. Many of the kids made fun of me when they found out that I was Jewish, taunting, "You killed Jesus!" At that time, I didn't even know who Jesus was! I later learned that my father was beaten up as a child and called a "dirty Jew" in his Brooklyn neighborhood. I remember feeling deeply embarrassed that I was Jewish, and I never wanted to talk about my heritage.

Because we lived in a non-Jewish community, it was very important to my father that we keep our Jewish identity. We drove forty-five minutes nearly every Friday night to Waterloo, Iowa, for a Sabbath service at a conservative synagogue. Almost every Sunday we also attended Sunday school to learn about the Jewish Holy Days and study the Old Covenant. At thirteen, I was confirmed into the Jewish faith and was given my very own copy of the Holy Scriptures. I did not, however, have a *Bat Mitzvah*, since at that time my parents were too busy to drive me during the week to study Hebrew, which was a requirement for a *Bat Mitzvah*.

Another reason that I feared my father was because I had no privacy. He could walk into my bedroom at any time without any warning. One such time I was sitting on my bed reading the Holy Scriptures, which is the Old Covenant (or Old Testament). My father assumed that I was reading the New Testament. He began punching me and yelling, "I will break every bone in your body if I ever catch you reading the New Testament again!" I tried to tell him that it was the Holy Scriptures, the Old Testament, but he would not believe me. After beating me, he flew into a rage, ripped the posters off of my bedroom walls, and slammed the door as hard as he could.

My father never apologized or even listened to me when I tried to tell him that he was wrong. This "bruised reed" felt like it had been broken. I cried myself to sleep that night, once again wishing that I was dead. My depression was exacerbated by the fact that my father made us pretend that Esther was dead because she had married a non-Jew. My mother didn't truly agree with this decision but felt powerless to challenge my father. I became increasingly more withdrawn and had nightmares about my sister Esther. I still remember dreaming that she was walking towards the hospital, and my father made her leave the hospital grounds.

I began to have difficulty concentrating in high school, and would daydream about Esther. In my mind and heart I could not resolve her absence in our lives. I knew that I needed to confront my father, to tell him that I didn't think it was fair that he required me to disown Esther. After all, she was my sister, and I needed to have a relationship with her. With fear and trepidation, I walked into his office after school one day to tell him that I needed my sister in my life. With all the courage I could muster, I proceeded to tell him how her absence had affected me, and that I felt like I needed to see her. Much to my surprise, he heard me and agreed that it was unfair for him to expect me to disown her just because he had. He encouraged me to contact her, and then made arrangements for me to fly out and visit her in Connecticut. He made it very clear, however, that I was not to talk to Mom or him about Esther or her husband when I returned. Looking back and recognizing issues that

I have had with authority figures, I realize that this was one of my first victories in facing those issues.

The reunion was a glorious occasion. By that time Esther had given birth to her first child, a little boy named Joey. It felt like a scene right out of a movie, and it was a great joy to meet her husband Joe and my new nephew. When I came home, I offered to show my father pictures. At first he declined. However, later he approached me with the idea that since he was a psychiatrist, he could look at the pictures from that standpoint, but not as her father.

I felt much better that I was allowed to have a relationship with my sister in spite of my parents' decision to disown her. The following summer, I asked to visit Esther again, but my father refused. He suggested instead that if Esther and her family wanted to visit Cathy and me, that perhaps they could come to Iowa – but they would not be welcome to stay with us. He recommended they camp out at one of the local campgrounds, and gave Cathy and me permission to visit them there. When I called Esther and told her about Dad's idea, she and her husband jumped at the chance to see us. They loved to camp, so they agreed to make the trip out west with their camper. After they had arrived and settled in, since my father did not want to even set eyes on them, they picked up Cathy and me at the edge of the hospital grounds.

One afternoon, as we were sitting at the picnic table, I thought about all the hurt and rejection Esther had suffered at the hands of my parents. I asked her what she would do if my parents ever decided to invite her back into our family. I was amazed by her reaction. She stated that because she realized what it would take for them to humble themselves, she would forgive them completely. Minutes later, I saw a car approaching and exclaimed, "Boy, that sure looks like Mom and Dad's car!" Sure enough, my parents got out of the car and walked towards us! I felt like I was dreaming. Could this really be happening after all this time? Could we ever become a family again? The next few minutes will be forever etched in my memory. There were embraces, tears, and of course introductions as Mom and Dad finally met Esther's husband Joe and their first grandson, Joey.

I later learned that it was my mother's idea to come to the campsite to see Esther. She had told my father that life was too short, and that he needed to accept her back into the family along with her husband and child.

My parents immediately invited Esther and Joe to pack up the camper and come back to our apartment to stay with the family during their visit. Dad and Joe seemed to hit it off quite well, perhaps because they were both in the mental health field. What a happy reunion! To top it off, the next day my father took them all around the hospital and introduced them to as many people as he could find! It was as though nothing had ever happened. Esther forgave them immediately, just as she had said she would.

When Esther was first disowned, I realized that my father only loved us conditionally. As long as we did everything according to his plan for us, as long as we obeyed him completely, we would be loved. If not, we risked losing his love. Perhaps this set the stage for my distorted view that God the Father loves us conditionally, only when we are obedient.

It wouldn't be long before my own rebellion would surface, further testing this conditional love from my father. But for now, I retreated further into my private fantasy world, hoping and praying that someday this bruised reed would recover and thrive.

Exploring Chapter 1

My Thoughts

No matter what suffering we experience in our family of origin, there is hope. The Lord knows the end from the beginning, and is weaving His threads of love into the fabric of our lives. I did not know His love at this time, but there was a day coming when He would reveal to me that He had indeed been working behind the scenes on my behalf all the time.

Your Turn

Do you identify with anything in my childhood story? How has your relationship with your parents impacted the way you view your Heavenly Father?

Chapter 2
Chasing After the Wind

*"I have seen all the things that are done under the sun;
all of them are meaningless, a chasing after the wind."*
Ecclesiastes 1:14

*M*y mother always had a great sense of adventure, and she passed this trait along to her three daughters. We all love to travel and to this day we all really love adventure.

When I was in ninth grade, my mother became our Girl Scout leader. I have many happy memories of camping trips, working on our badges, and weekend bake sales. But most exciting was the year my mother thought it would be fun if we started saving all our money from Girl Scout cookies and bake sales to earn enough to take a trip to Europe. I was a senior in high school, and we worked very hard to raise $600 each, which enabled our Girl Scout troop to take a three-week trip to nine countries in Europe in the summer of 1967. What a great graduation gift for everyone in our troop! My younger sister Cathy came along too, and Dad decided that he would meet us in Paris and spend a few days touring with us. The local newspaper did a feature article on our trip, and when we returned home we were treated like celebrities. My mother was a wonderful Girl Scout leader, and those were happy times during my teenage years living in the hospital in Independence, Iowa.

During my high school years I had led a very sheltered life, and I was never allowed to date. Because we were the only Jewish family in Independence, Iowa, and my parents' desire was for me to marry within our faith, they did not want me to associate too closely with non-Jewish kids. Thus, when I went away to college, I had no idea what awaited me. My parents had not explained the consequences of sexual activity outside of marriage, and, starved for love, I fell prey to any guy who showed attention to me.

I attended Drake University in Des Moines, Iowa, majoring in music education. My college years were the era of the sixties revolution. The philosophies of the day included "Do your own thing!" "Make love, not war!" "Peace!" "Rebel against the establishment!" and "Expand your mind with drugs!" Searching for meaning in unchartered territory with no concept of the consequences, I began "chasing after the wind".

I was vulnerable and wanted nothing more than to be accepted by my peers. I started skipping classes and hung out in communes and coffeehouses. This was during the Vietnam War years, and there were many political rallies and anti-war demonstrations on campus. I took an active role, and became immersed in the culture of the day. Since my parents had no idea that I was involved in this subversive lifestyle, I was leading a double life. The mental institute where I had grown up was only about a hundred miles from college, and whenever I went home to visit, I made sure that I showered well. I donned my normal clothes, leaving the bell-bottoms and tie-dyed shirts back at school.

It was becoming increasingly difficult to live in two opposing worlds, but I felt there was no turning back. I had made a lot of friends and was very popular, unlike high school where I felt like a rejected wallflower. I dabbled in the occult, at first innocently with the Ouiji Board. At that time I had no idea that evil was real, and that Satan, the fallen angel, ruled the darkness. Once I opened the door to this unseen realm, my fascination was piqued. I began attending séances and stepped deeper into the occult, having no idea where this was leading me. I didn't realize that I had unleashed an evil presence in my life.

Due to my occult involvement, I began having nightmares and saw dark shadowy figures in my room at night. I had no idea that I had opened myself up to this dark and frightening world. I started using more drugs so I could sleep at night and escape further.

Years later, even after I came to know the Lord, the forces of darkness still had a forceful and controlling grip on me. I realized that I needed help to break free from the powers of darkness associated with the occult. I received very strong deliverance prayer, and the Lord set me free. I have never again been tempted to return to this dark and scary world of the occult.

In my sophomore year of college a friend handed me a tiny pill and told me that if I took it, I would have a wonderful spiritual experience. I didn't question him, and gladly received it. I didn't know at the time that it was LSD, a very powerful hallucinogenic drug.

Ever since I can remember, I have been able to recall my dreams, vividly, in color, and very realistic. I've always had a very active imagination, so that when I took LSD, I went completely into another realm. I felt as though I was in another galaxy, and lost complete touch with reality. There was one whole week at school that I could not account for. While I was under the influence of LSD, I had sent out an application to Western Michigan University in Kalamazoo, Michigan to transfer and switch my major from music education to music therapy. I had absolutely no recollection that I had sent the application until I received the letter of acceptance in the mail. At that time in my life, everything was a "sign", so I took that as an opportunity to make a change.

Having no idea whatsoever that I was leading a double life, my parents approved of the change of college and continued to pay for my education. They paid for me to live in a dormitory, but because I was embroiled in the hippie lifestyle, it didn't take me long to find the hippies on campus. Before long, I was invited to join a commune. I kept my dorm room for appearance's sake, but I had really moved into the commune. Our commune was a stopping place for drug dealers, so we always managed to get free drugs. I became more sexually promiscuous, and began hitchhiking to anti-war rallies all over the country. I had no idea at the time that my own father was appearing in Senate sub-committee hearings to lobby against the use of illegal drugs. If he only knew ...

As I became more and more irresponsible, my grades began to slip. I gained quite a bit of weight, and was rapidly losing my sense of self. I had such a desperate need to feel loved and accepted by my peers that I would do whatever they asked of me.

When I was twenty, I went in for a routine gynecological visit. The doctor did a series of blood tests that revealed, to my horror, that I was pregnant! When the nurse called me into the office to tell me, I began swearing at her, telling her she was insane, that there was no possible way I could be pregnant! I had never used any form of contraception, yet somehow believed that I was immune to pregnancy!

It took a while for reality to sink in, and by the time I came to terms with my pregnancy, I was already well into my second trimester. I felt despondent. I knew that if I told my parents, they would surely disown me. Their acceptance meant too much to me, and I could not risk losing their love.

I felt I had no choice. Abortion seemed the only way to stop my growing fear. I was completely self-centered and was terrified of the day that I would begin to show and my parents would find out that I was pregnant. Abortion seemed the only answer – but this was prior to the 1973 Roe vs. Wade case that legalized abortion nationwide. Abortion was still illegal in Michigan, and was also illegal in most states. Then I found out that abortion was legal in California. It seemed my only way out. I pleaded with my friends to help me. I knew nothing about making an adoption plan.

My friends came to the rescue and began selling some of their possessions to help pay for my trip to California and the ensuing abortion. I flew out to California where the abortion would be performed in a hospital clinic. The people in the hospital made arrangements for me to stay in a motel with another girl who was also getting an abortion, so we could share expenses.

In those days, the California law required that before I could be granted the abortion, I had to appear before a panel of three professionals to prove to them that I should be considered an unfit mother. If they agreed, I would be granted the abortion. One of the people on the panel was a psychiatrist.

I managed to convince them that I was too depressed and unsure of myself to even imagine becoming a mother at this stage of my life. I told them about my father and that he would disown me. They agreed to grant me the abortion, but with the caveat that I would never allow this to happen again. They didn't even speak to me about abstaining from sexual activity, but instead suggested that I take birth control pills. I agreed.

They called the procedure a "therapeutic abortion", and required me to check into the hospital. Because I was in the second trimester, I was told that they would perform a saline abortion. This meant that they would inject a highly concentrated salt solution into the uterus that would poison the fetus so that it would die, and then they would give me medication so that I would give birth to the dead baby. I remember the nurse telling me to press the call button when I felt the baby stop kicking. The end of his kicking would indicate that he was dead, and it was time to induce labor. I was told that I would experience labor pains similar to live birth.

Although the panel of three professionals used the word "fetus", the nurse in the hospital used the word "baby". I was shocked, because I had been told by the doctor performing the abortion that it was "just a mass of tissue". There was a woman in the bed next to mine, also having an abortion. Even today her screams still ring in my ears, "My baby! My baby!"

By the time I pushed the baby out, I was quite numb and did not allow myself to feel the emotional pain too deeply. I soon entered a time of denial that persisted for many years.

I needed to get out of California as soon as possible and get back to school so no one would suspect anything was wrong. On the plane back to Michigan, I began to feel pain in my body. I was concerned that something must have gone wrong with the abortion. As soon as I arrived home, I called a doctor. However, when I told the doctor that I had had an abortion, since I was under the age of 21, he refused to examine me without my parent's permission. His decision to deny me care was fueled by the fact that abortion was illegal in Michigan. He was unwilling to treat me in the event that there were any complications.

The pain worsened, and I began taking more illicit drugs to try to quell it. I had gained even more weight and was having flashbacks and nightmares. I had no idea that I was suffering from the traumatic effects of the abortion, today known as Post-Abortion Syndrome.

Eventually, I couldn't even concentrate in school, and when I was performing before a music jury, I completely lost my place in the music. I received a failing grade in my major performance instrument, the saxophone. I knew my parents would eventually find out that I failed, but I didn't know what to do. In a panic, I called my sister Esther, living with her husband Joe in Connecticut.

When I told her about the abortion, she insisted that I officially drop out of school and fly out to Connecticut so that I could stay with them. She assured me that they would do whatever they could to get me the help I needed.

When I arrived, she saw how much pain I was experiencing and called the local hospital. When she told them that I had had an abortion, they too told her that without my parent's consent, they could not examine me. At that point, my sister insisted that I call Mom and Dad and tell them what had happened.

I finally decided that my sister was right. I had built a wall around my heart to protect me from their certain rejection, so I had nothing to lose at that point. Overcome with physical and emotional pain, I felt numb and scared. What could possibly be any worse? I picked up the phone and, with trembling hands, dialed their number. I was astounded at the conversation that followed.

"Daddy, I was pregnant and had an abortion."

Dad yelled into the receiver, "What did you say? You were pregnant and had an abortion? How could you do this to us? You might as well kill yourself! You are no more use to this family!" He slammed the phone down, and at that moment I realized that I was right. My father loved me conditionally, only when I was a good little girl. I had known this was going to happen. I was living my worst nightmare.

But minutes later, much to my surprise, the phone rang again. My father had a much softer and compassionate tone. His words penetrated deeply into my heart and soul. "Janie, I love you. I am going to fly your mother out to Connecticut and we will get you help. I'll call the hospital right now and give them permission to examine you."

At that moment, I could scarcely breathe. Was this real or a fairy tale? Was I going to wake up and realize that I had only hoped I would hear those words? It took a few minutes, but I realized that my father had actually said the words that I had so longed to hear. I thanked him, and Esther immediately drove me to the hospital to be examined. All of a sudden I realized that as soon as I heard those words, "Janie, I love you," all the pain that I had been feeling in my body since the abortion completely disappeared! When the doctor examined me, he found absolutely nothing wrong and discharged me right away.

I eventually realized that the fear of being rejected by my father caused the intense pain in my body. I am sure that the extreme anxiety I was feeling and the post-abortion stress exacerbated the situation as well.

Within a couple days, my mother arrived. She was obviously shaken and hurt, and I still felt pretty numb. Our relationship had always been distant and cold, and we knew very little about each other. We found we didn't really know how to relate to each other.

My father had arranged for us to meet with one of the top psychiatrists on the east coast. I expected that this psychiatrist would rake me over the coals. I fully believed the lie that I was a really bad person.

We walked into his plush office, and my mother proceeded to tell him all the terrible things I had done to bring shame on our family. She explained that she and my father felt betrayed and humiliated. How would my father explain this to his colleagues and the rest of our family? According to my mother, my father believed that I would never be a useful member to society. His plan was to have me move back home, possibly get admitted to the hospital and be treated by a psychiatrist on his staff. I said nothing. Full of shame, I kept my head down. I knew that whatever I said would be held against me, so I kept my mouth shut. After about thirty minutes, the psychiatrist told my mother that he wanted to meet with me alone.

To my surprise, he asked me how I was feeling. I had difficulty answering that question, because I had become quite adept at hiding my feelings. I also did not feel safe. He asked again, and in a very quiet and tentative voice I replied, "Scared." He then caught me completely off guard with his response.

"I can see the amount of pressure that you're under, and can only imagine how you must be feeling. And I disagree with your father. I don't believe it would be in your best interest to live at home. I think you need to regain your sense of self. Your father has a very tight hold on you, and in order for you to grow and mature into a healthy adult, I will recommend that you do not return to live with your parents but remain on the east coast. I will set you up with one of my colleagues for intensive psychoanalytic therapy. Perhaps your parents can arrange for you to live with a relative. This probably will be met with some resistance on your father's part, but I will personally phone him and tell him the rationale for my recommendation. How does that sound to you?"

This was certainly not the response I expected to hear! At first I thought I had lost touch with reality and was only imagining this conversation. But when I looked up and saw his compassionate smile, I knew that it was genuine. I hesitated for a moment and then answered, "I guess that would be just fine."

My heart was beating a mile a minute. How would my father take this news? Would he make me go home? I knew that if he did, I would probably die inside. I was not crazy, and I didn't think my father's idea to admit me to his mental hospital was sound at all. I would only get worse if he made me come home. My thoughts were interrupted when the doctor announced that our time was up and that he would be contacting my father. He advised me to not say anything to my mother until he had personally spoken to my father.

I kept my tentative feelings of relief inside as I left his office with my mother. She did not initiate conversation, and neither did I. We went straight to her sister Henrietta's house in West Hartford, Connecticut.

As soon as we opened the door, Aunt Henri announced that my father had called and wanted my mother to call him back as soon as possible. My mother went into another room to return his call, and I did not hear their conversation. About ten minutes later, my mother emerged. She asked Aunt Henri if she could speak with her alone, and they left the room. Once again, I was left with a whirlwind of thoughts. Did the psychiatrist talk to my father? Were they going to put me on the next plane home? Does my Aunt Henri hate me now?

Eventually they both came back into the living room with confused looks on their faces. Mom told me that my father had spoken to the psychiatrist, and that he had recommended that I stay on the east coast and meet with one of his colleagues for intensive psychoanalytical therapy. Mom went on to say that she had asked Aunt Henri if I could live with her family while I was receiving therapy. Many summers I had come to visit them, and I had a wonderful relationship with Aunt Henri, Uncle

Paul, and my cousins Ellen, Chipper, and Johnny. They all welcomed me to live with them without hesitation, and strangely, I felt closer to them than my own family. I was overjoyed inside, but still too afraid to show it.

A couple days later, my mother flew back to Iowa. My aunt and uncle had decided that I could help them in their art framing business, since I was too anxious and depressed to hold down a paying job at that point in time.

I began my first session with the psychiatrist the following week. I would be meeting with him three times a week. Prior to our meeting he explained to my aunt and uncle that I would be experiencing many different emotions, and that my moods could change drastically from day to day. He wanted to normalize my experience for them so that they wouldn't be alarmed at my extreme mood swings.

The psychiatrist gave me the diagnosis of anxious neurotic and did not prescribe any psychotropic medication. Since the therapy was psychoanalytic in nature, the role of the therapist was passive. For the most part, I would walk in, sit down, and begin. There were no occasions for small talk and very few questions or prodding on his part. I kept a faithful journal for the first year, after which time the psychiatrist asked me to stop. He felt I was writing too much and our sessions were not as productive. There had been many times that I came into his office and for the entire forty-five minutes did not utter one word. We sat in silence until the time was up.

Recently, I pulled out that journal and read the entries. The level of confusion and lack of insight I experienced that first year into the process was shocking. I also saw that I had expressed a great deal of anger towards my father. Much of my work with the psychiatrist that first year was geared toward helping me to find my own voice and preparing me to stand up to my father.

One session toward the end of our first year together stands out in my mind. I told him how concerned I was about what my father thought of me. This is the only time I remember my doctor taking an active role. He stood up and with a loud booming voice exclaimed, "When are you going to stop living the life your father wants for you? You need to find out who you are and live your own life. At this moment, he is working, and not concerned about what you're doing. It's about time you stand up to him and realize that you have a voice and that what you feel matters!"

I remember exactly how I felt at that moment, and exactly what I thought: *It really is okay for me to have my own feelings, no matter what my father thinks.* For the first time in my life, I began to think that I could have the courage to stand up to him and tell him how I felt!!

I now know that the doctor was empowering me by giving me permission to reclaim lost ground. He was helping me to individuate, to find out who I am apart from my parents. We set a goal that in one month, when my parents were coming to visit, I would confront my father. I would tell him that I was upset that he was unwilling to pay back my friends for the money they gave me for the trip to California and the abortion. I was getting stronger and would soon be able to work, and I wanted to ask him for a loan to pay them back. I felt that it was the right thing to do. I was scared and worried about his potential reaction, but I knew in my heart that I needed to speak directly to him, or risk further loss of self.

As the time for my parent's visit was looming large, the psychiatrist continued to provide me with hope. He encouraged me to let go of my fear and begin thinking of myself as a young woman with goals, hopes, and dreams. I knew that I had nothing to lose, but everything to gain.

I needed to see my father as a human being, not as a mean ogre who was out to get me. After all, he too was a psychiatrist, and knew all about people who suffer from mental anguish. I could only hope he would show some empathy towards his own daughter.

Exploring Chapter 2

My Thoughts

Even though I was living a double life while in college, deep inside I knew it was wrong. I believe I was looking for a way out of my hippie lifestyle, but at that time my self-esteem was at an all time low. I could see no means of escape. Perhaps the crisis of my abortion, which forced me to tell my parents the truth, was my way out, my pathway towards normalcy.

Your Turn

Was there ever a time in your life when what seemed like a horrible time actually turned out to be the way out?

Chapter 3
Reclaiming Lost Ground

"Fear of man will prove to be a snare,
but whoever trusts in the Lord is kept safe."

Proverbs 29:25

The week before the arrival of my parents, the psychiatrist continued to build up my confidence. He reiterated over and over again that I had nothing to fear, other than possible rejection. He kept assuring me that if that were to happen, I could live through it. I endured many days and nights filled with fear and anxiety, but somehow I managed to cling to the words of the psychiatrist.

The day my parents drove up the driveway to my aunt and uncle's house, for a fleeting moment I wanted to run out the back door and forget about the whole thing. However, as though some untapped inner strength began welling up inside of me, I suddenly knew that I was going to do just fine.

My parents warmly greeted the family and tentatively approached me. With tears in my eyes I hugged them. Very few words were spoken at that moment. They were offered drinks and began getting caught up on all the news with my aunt and uncle.

After what seemed like an eternity, I asked my father if we could talk privately. He followed me onto the porch, and when we sat down, I began to speak with strength and confidence.

I told him how I had felt that his love was conditional all throughout my childhood. I shared how it hurt me deeply the way he treated Esther and me, and how he never gave us a chance to defend ourselves. I went on to say how hard it was to live with the threat of rejection, and how it seemed that I could do nothing right. I told him that I knew my hippie lifestyle hurt him very deeply, and that I regretted the poor decisions I had made. However, I wanted him to know that my friends had stood by me and helped me when I decided to have the abortion, and I didn't think it was fair not to pay them back. I asked him to loan me the money so that I could send it back to them.

There were a few moments of silence, and then, much to my surprise, my father took out his check book and started asking me to whom should he write the checks out, and for how much! He told me I would need to pay him back when I was able to begin working again. I ran into his arms, crying and thanking him profusely. With a bounce in my step and a renewed hope, I suggested we walk to the mailbox together.

Both my father and I have a very poor sense of direction, and many of the streets and houses in the neighborhood looked very similar. We mailed the checks, and got lost trying to find our way back home. Over an hour later, my mom and Aunt Henri realized that we were probably lost, and drove around until they found us. A bit of levity was most welcome at this point in time. We all had a wonderful laugh, and I treasure that memory.

The talk with my father was a huge epiphany as I began to face my "fear of man" issues. Our relationship was beginning to heal, and he later told me how much he respected me for standing up to him. The rest of the visit was warm and peaceful. I believe that I was beginning to experience who I was apart from my parents, and the process of family differentiation had begun.

I had never been allowed to have a voice in my family,

so standing up to my father for the first time in my life made me feel like I was reclaiming lost ground from long ago. The next session with my psychiatrist was extremely productive, and he affirmed the courage it took for me to finally stand up to my father and reclaim that lost ground. I had begun to find my voice. For the first time in my life I was beginning to feel hopeful that maybe I truly *was* a woman of value, maybe what I had to say *was* important, and perhaps I *could* accomplish my dreams and goals.

After several more sessions, the psychiatrist felt that it was time for me to become more independent. I had been in therapy for over a year, and he recommended that I begin pursuing a low stress job and eventually move out on my own. He suggested that we meet one time a week instead of three. This was a real affirmation of the progress I had made in therapy.

I saw an advertisement in the paper for a receptionist, a "Girl Friday" in a plant that distributed plastic dishes. I went in for an interview, and was shocked when the next day I was offered the job. The owner was a very kind man and was quite patient with me as I learned the mechanics of the work. I connected well with everyone, and actually enjoyed working there.

After a few months, I moved into a boarding house where I had my own room, and shared common areas with other boarders. I decorated my room myself. I bought a black light, painted the ceiling black, and also purchased a tapestry with a picture of Jesus. At that time in my life I didn't know much about Jesus, but somehow I felt connected to Him, sensing His presence and care. Even though about the only thing I knew was that, as Jews, we were not supposed to believe in Jesus, I still felt that in some way He was protecting me from unseen dangers. His picture on the tapestry brought me a sense of comfort and peace.

One January day in 1971, when I was 21, two men came in to service the plant's oil burner. I was immediately attracted to the younger of the two men. He didn't seem to notice me, and I assumed that he was stuck up. My co-workers explained that he was just shy. In my impatience, I eventually took matters into my own hands and introduced myself to him. I later learned that the older man had encouraged him to talk to me, but I had addressed him before he even had a chance to initiate.

It didn't take me long to obtain some critical information during that first encounter. I found out that his name was Dave and that he still lived at home. He did not have a girlfriend at that time, which was definitely a plus. He was two years younger than me, which didn't bother me in the least! We hit it off right away, and I invited him to visit me sometime. I gave him my address, and had a feeling he might come to see me that same night. I had a boyfriend that I didn't like anymore, and as soon I got home that day, I told him he had to leave and take all of his belongings with him. About one hour later, there was a knock on the door, and it was Dave! My heart skipped a beat as I opened the door. We felt comfortable and safe with each other immediately. I didn't realize it right away, but I had finally found my true soul mate.

We began to talk, and although our family backgrounds were very different, there was a deep connection. Dave came from an Italian blue-collar family. Dave's father had been brought up in the south in a very strict Pentecostal home. Dave's grandfather was physically abusive, so Dave's father decided to enter the service to escape his wrath.

Dave's mother came from an Italian Catholic family with many siblings. Her father and stepmother were both physically abusive, so when Dave's father came into the picture, she was glad to escape their wrath.

After they wed, Dave's father converted to Catholicism since that was very important to his new bride. They decided the children would be raised Catholic as well.

There were four children in the family. When Dave was two, his one-year-old sister died from viral pneumonia. Dave's parents carried the pain of this tragedy all throughout their married life.

Dave's father eventually admitted that he was a compulsive gambler. When Dave was 23, his mother gave his father an ultimatum. Dave's father went to Gamblers Anonymous and there received hope, became free from gambling, and remained free for the rest of his life! He made amends to family and friends, and we are all very proud of him!

One thing that Dave and I shared in common was the fact that both of our fathers were abusive. There were many times that Dave was beaten and misunderstood by his father. I think that perhaps the pressures associated with trying to hide his addiction contributed to the anger and rage that his father unleashed upon Dave and even more so upon Dave's older brother.

It took Dave quite a while before he was ready to introduce me to his family. He was concerned that because our faith and our ethnic backgrounds were so different, it might be awkward. I assured him that I would love to meet his family and didn't care about the difference in our backgrounds.

Dave decided that Thanksgiving would be a good time, so he invited me to their family dinner. I was very nervous, wondering whether or not they would like me, especially since I was not Catholic. In those days it was very important to marry someone with the same faith. When I arrived, Dave's mother was upset because the electricity had gone off for a while and the turkey was not yet ready. Nevertheless, it was easy to see that his family was close knit and cared for one another. They were down-to-earth with absolutely no pretenses, and I immediately felt welcomed into their family. It saddened me to admit this, but in many ways I felt closer to Dave's parents than my own.

Dave and I continued to date, and I had a feeling that he was the man I would one day marry. I waited for an opportunity to introduce Dave to my family, which offered quite a challenge in view of their stance on intermarriage. I was in no hurry!

Dave, like me, had experimented with hallucinogenic drugs. A few months into our relationship, he had a very bad experience with drugs. He thought he heard God telling him that if he used another drug that he would die. That was enough to scare him, and he never picked up another illegal drug again. We were both determined to leave the hippie lifestyle behind, and as we did, our relationship continued to blossom.

I continued to progress in therapy, but by this time I was 23, and my father had stopped paying for my therapy. It was up to me if I wanted to continue. I was not making a huge salary, and I sent most of my money to my father to pay back the loan he had given me to repay my friends. I scheduled therapy on a less frequent basis, and began feeling that after three years I was ready to end therapy. I felt as though I had made significant progress in my ability to individuate and gain autonomy from my parents. I actually had a desire to complete my college education and perhaps major in Therapeutic Recreation. I had volunteered in Therapeutic Recreation many summers at the state hospital and had really enjoyed it.

When I told my psychiatrist about my desire, he was very encouraging and supportive. However, he didn't think at that point I was ready to end therapy completely.

I told him I would continue, but that if I got accepted at a university, I would be leaving the area.

I sent applications to two schools offering the program I was interested in pursuing. One was in the state of Washington, and the other in Minnesota. My GPA was not very high because of my irresponsible lifestyle, but I was still hopeful. I submitted the application and waited for a return reply. Would it be a thick or a thin envelope? Every day I checked the mail, hoping against hope.

Then one day, to my delight, I received a thick envelope from Mankato State College in Minnesota. I had been accepted and had also qualified for a low interest student loan. My parents were not going to help me financially this time around since I had elected to drop out before I graduated.

My next hurdle was to convince Dave to pull up stakes and go out west with me. Since he had only ever lived in Hartford, Connecticut, and had not traveled much, it would be quite an adventure for him, and perhaps a chance to begin a new life.

To my surprise, it was not hard to convince Dave. We loved each other, and he was ready for a change. I told my psychiatrist that we would be leaving soon, and we began the termination process. Even though my psychiatrist felt that I wasn't ready to end therapy, he wished me the best and affirmed the wonderful gains I had made over our three years together. He was a very kind and compassionate man, and I will always be grateful to him for helping me find my voice.

It was hard to say good-bye to Dave's family, and to Aunt Henri and her wonderful family who had done so much for me during those tumultuous years. It was very painful, but everyone encouraged us to proceed. Before we moved, we flew out to Mankato, Minnesota to find a place to live. I also wanted to get familiar with the campus. We found a beautiful basement apartment that faced a pretty lake. It was modern, furnished, and within our budget – and there was even a fireplace. We put down a deposit and headed back to Connecticut to begin packing.

In the fall of 1972, we loaded everything we owned into a U-Haul and left the east coast, making the long drive out west. Dave was 21, and I was 23. In many ways it felt like a real adventure. What would our lives be like? Only God knew, and hopefully He would fill us in!

We planned to stop in Michigan en route so I could see some old friends from college. I wanted them to meet Dave, and it seemed like a good place to rest before making our way to Minnesota. It was fun to introduce Dave to my friends. The last time they had seen me was just before I had dropped out of college. They were pleased to see the change in my life.

Minnesota was a bit of a culture shock, especially for Dave. The commercials on television often featured polka music and advertisements about farm machinery. There was not much diversity in the culture. It seemed that almost everyone had blonde hair and blue eyes and that their last name was either Johnson or Anderson! There was a large Norwegian and Swedish population in Mankato, and since I am blonde, I was almost always mistaken for a Norwegian or a Swede. People were shocked when I told them that I was Jewish! The restaurants were all fairly similar, mostly "cake and steak houses" or pizzerias that served cracker-thin pizza. This made Dave pine for good New England pizza. But by far, the hardest adjustment was the weather.

It was extremely cold in the winter. Some days in January barely reached zero degrees, and the wind chill factor was much lower. We eventually bought a used car, and Dave spent too much time outdoors having to fix it. One day he came in with icicles on his mustache! At night we needed to plug in our car heater so that the engine would not freeze up! There was snow, and plenty of it. A twenty-inch snowstorm was not unusual at all. What was surprising was the fact that there were virtually no snow days, because the city was extremely well prepared to handle large volumes of snow. This undoubtedly disappointed the kids! In the spring it was not uncommon to still see huge snowdrifts several feet high all along the sides of the major highways and city streets. It didn't melt until sometime in April, and spring was a very short season.

Summer was very hot and humid because of Minnesota's 20,000 lakes. Even worse were the mosquitoes. Residents affectionately referred to the mosquito as the "Minnesota State Bird"! But eventually, we acclimated.

The people were known in the region as "Minnesota nice". Minnesotans were almost always very pleasant, but you never quite knew what they were really thinking. Sometimes, the nice was just a façade. People might "act nice" even if they felt differently, and seemed reluctant to tell others how they really felt.

In college, I took the maximum number of credits so that I could graduate in one year. Thankfully, all of my other credits from the other two universities transferred. I worked part time as a waitress at a local Holiday Inn restaurant to help pay expenses.

Dave tried for several months to get a job in Mankato, but was unsuccessful. In those days, Dave had long hair and a beard. He would see advertisements in the paper, or job signs in the window, and as soon as the owners saw him approaching, the signs would be whisked away. The next day he would drive by and notice that the signs were back. On principle, Dave was unwilling to cut his hair and beard. He didn't think he should be judged for his outward appearance. However, we learned that in that town there had been some riots between the "hippies" and "rednecks". His long hair and beard was probably a turn off to the small town shop owners.

Day after day, Dave kept searching for a job. In desperation, he even applied to wash dishes in a Shakey's Pizza restaurant. The shop owner had mercy on Dave, and told him that as long as he stayed in the kitchen out of public view, he was hired. Little did we know that this job would open up a whole new chapter in our lives.

> *"I will lead the blind by ways they have not known,*
> *along unfamiliar paths I will guide them;*
> *I will turn the darkness into light before them*
> *and make the rough places smooth.*
> *These are the things I will do;*
> *I will not forsake them."*   Isaiah 42:16

Exploring Chapter 3

My Thoughts

Sometimes facing our greatest fear is the first step towards wellness. Because I had supportive people in my life that believed in me, I had the courage to face my fear and confront my father. I knew that I would grow as a person if I took this risk. Looking back, this was the very beginning of my ability to trust God in the unknown and step out in faith.

Your Turn

Think of a time when you faced an overwhelming fear. How were you able to overcome it?

Chapter 4
A New Creation!

"I led them with cords of human kindness,
with ties of love.
To them I was like one who lifts
a little child to the cheek,
and I bent down to feed them."   Hosea 11:4

t age 24, I graduated from college with a Bachelor of Science in Parks and Recreation with a special emphasis in Therapeutic Recreation, and also a minor in Music. The year was 1973. I was offered a position as a Recreation Therapist at a nursing home. But before I could accept it, another opportunity presented itself ...

Dave was still employed at Shakey's Pizza Parlor. Every weekend Shakey's had live music featuring a Honky Tonk piano player, whom I will call "Sam". Dave and the pianist struck up a friendship. When Sam learned that Dave had been taking flute lessons, he offered Dave an occasional opportunity to bring his flute and "sit in". Sam then offered to teach him the upright bass. Soon, Dave sold our car cassette player in order to purchase a bass. When Dave and I and the bass piled into our little Chevy, I found myself squeezed into a tiny corner in the back seat, "playing second fiddle" to the upright bass!

Eventually, Sam asked Dave if he wanted to form a

band and go on the road. When Sam learned that I had a music background and had studied voice in college, he offered me the position of lead singer. He coached both of us for quite a while, then just as I graduated, he advertised our availability. I was in a quandary since I had just been offered a position in my field of study. However, I had always had a dream to be a professional singer, and I knew that if I walked away from this opportunity, I would always wonder what I might have missed. So I turned down the position as Recreational Therapist in the nursing home, and the next thing I knew we were getting our promo materials together and forming our band, *The Honky Tonk Revival*. Dave was known as "Mr. Downbeat", and I was the "Queen of the Revival".

At first it was very exciting. Sam bought a motor home, which would be our home away from home as we traveled. We procured several gigs in various supper clubs and even in a Playboy Club in Wisconsin. We drove across several states and found campgrounds to park our motor home. Since our gigs were at night, we would sleep until late morning, and then get up and prepare our meals and rest before the next night's gig.

It became obvious to me that this life was not as glamorous as I initially thought it would be. Sam was an alcoholic and a philanderer. The drummer also drank, although the banjo player was a family man who drove to the gigs on his own and was not a drinker. Shortly after we began our tour, it became obvious that Sam was interested in a physical relationship with me. He was a married man, but he convinced me that there was nothing wrong with it since Dave and I were only living together and not married. I was vulnerable and extremely insecure. I fell for his charm, and we began an affair. He let me know that there were other women, but it never occurred to him that he needed to remain faithful to his wife. Our liaison went on for almost a year, and even though I knew deep inside it was wrong, I couldn't seem to end it. I hid it from Dave, and pretended everything was fine between us.

As time went along, I became depressed and began to wonder where my life was going. Since we were playing to a bunch of drunks who couldn't care less about the music, the gigs were completely unfulfilling. I was 25, and I was beginning to think about my life and wonder where I was headed. I began to question if this was all there was to life, and if it was really worth living. I could see that Sam was just using me, but I was already emotionally involved. I also began thinking about how I had worked so hard in college to finally win my degree, how I had spent so much money for tuition, and how I had now abandoned my career. The thoughts pressing in were overwhelming.

One day, I felt a sudden urge to leave the campgrounds and run into the woods to get away. I didn't know what was driving me, but I just knew that I had to be alone. I found a grassy spot, and laid face down. In my Jewish faith, I was never taught that God is personal, and I was never encouraged to pray other than corporately in the synagogue. So I was surprised to hear my own voice cry out loudly to the God of Abraham, Isaac, and Jacob. I told Him that if He was real, He had better reveal Himself to me, or otherwise I wanted to die.

I didn't see lightning bolts or hear thunderclaps, but all of a sudden I felt this deep peace envelop me. Intuitively, I knew my prayer had been answered – but I was not sure what that meant. Jeremiah says,

"You will seek me and find me when you search for me with all your heart." Jeremiah 29:13 NASB

As I slowly stood up to prepare to return to the motor home, I knew beyond a shadow of a doubt that I needed to quit the band and go back to Mankato. I announced my decision to Dave and to the other band members, and soon made plans to head back home. Dave decided to continue working with the band since it was steady income.

I knew in my heart that I needed to end my relationship with Sam as well. At this point Dave still did not know about the liaison. Very gradually, I felt that something inside my heart was beginning to change. I was seeing the world differently, and began to know the difference between right and wrong. Shortly after my decision to leave the band, I ended the relationship with Sam, much to his dismay.

Soon after I arrived back home, I decided to volunteer at a local agency that reached out and offered help to kids who had fallen into difficulties with drugs. Since I had come out of that lifestyle, I felt compassion and a sense of camaraderie. Very soon after I started working there, I was particularly drawn to one of the volunteers; I'll call her "Ann". I was struck by the fact that she seemed to have a very deep sense of peace and an unusual joy that I had not seen in anyone before. One day I felt compelled to talk to her, but she left before I had a chance to ask her about getting together with me.

Dave did not have a gig that weekend, so he was home. Not surprisingly, we were not getting along very well. Ever since I quit the band there had been a lot of tension, and we were arguing quite a bit. I think both of us were beginning to wonder if we could stay together, though neither of us brought it up in conversation.

Because I felt the urgency to talk to Ann, I called the agency and they gave me her number. I tried calling her, but her roommate said she wasn't home. She went on to say that I could find her at the local Catholic Church since she was involved in a function there that night. I felt such an urgency to see her, but I didn't understand why at the time. Dave had left the Catholic faith long ago, but when I asked Dave if he would go with me, he surprised me with his yes. From today's vantage point, I see that the Lord had an awesome plan for our lives, and this evening marked the beginning of our amazing journey of faith.

"For I am confident of this very thing, that He who began a good work in you will perfect it until the day of Christ Jesus." Philippians 1:6 NASB

As we approached the church, we saw a Greyhound bus parked directly in front. The destination sign on the front of the bus read, "Heaven!" When we walked into the church, we thought that we had stepped into a whole different world.

A band up front was singing songs about Jesus, and as we looked around the room, we noticed that all these people seemed to have the same joy that I saw in Ann! They had their hands raised and were singing like angels. This was quite a contrast to our experience of singing with a bunch of drunks to a bunch of drunks! We weren't sure how the people at this church would receive us, Dave with his wild long hair and me in my bell-bottoms and tie-dyed shirt. But surprisingly, people warmly greeted us and seemed genuinely happy that we were there. At one point Dave and I were both moved to tears, and whispered to each other that perhaps God was missing from our lives all these years. Maybe it was time to open our hearts to the possibility that God exists.

We learned later that we had actually walked into an ecumenical prayer meeting with Charismatic Catholics, Lutherans, and Presbyterians. There was such a sense of acceptance, unity, and love – something neither Dave nor

I had ever experienced before in our respective places of worship. After the prayer meeting, I found Ann and asked if I could meet with her. I did know that she was a hair stylist, so I asked if she would be willing to cut my hair.

At last I would have the opportunity to ask Ann about her peace and joy. We went up to her apartment, and as she began cutting my hair, I inquired about her life. She proceeded to tell me that she had grown up in the Catholic faith, but didn't stay with it when she left home. Like me, she had been involved in the hippie movement, and had suffered from depression. She met someone from the Catholic Charismatic community who told her about Jesus. He explained that if she accepted Jesus into her life, she would be forever changed. She decided to listen to her friend and accepted Jesus as her Lord and Savior. She shared with me that immediately after accepting Jesus into her heart, everything changed. The depression lifted, and she was filled with a deep peace and joy that gave her a new sense of peace and purpose.

As a Jewish person, this was all very foreign to me. I remember my father explaining to me that Jews do not believe in Jesus, and that Jesus is not God. My father also told to me that our people were persecuted by people who believed in Jesus, so that people who believe in Jesus are not to be trusted. Unfortunately, many of our people perished at the hands of those who claimed to be Christians, in the Russian pogroms and the Spanish Inquisition, and even Hitler claimed that he believed in Jesus.

I told Ann that I could not embrace her belief in Jesus since I truly believed that He was our enemy. But I now know that when we are ready, He lifts the veil, and enables us to comprehend the truth.

Ann had a very childlike and simple faith, and asked the Lord to reveal the truth to me. She said a prayer and asked Him to speak through the pages of the Bible. It's interesting that the first passage He led her to was Isaiah 53:

"Who has believed our message?
*And to whom has the arm of the L*ORD *been revealed?*
For He grew up before Him like a tender shoot,
And like a root out of parched ground;
He has no stately form or majesty
That we should look upon Him,
Nor appearance that we should be attracted to Him.
He was despised and forsaken of men,
A man of sorrows and acquainted with grief;
And like one from whom men hide their face
He was despised, and we did not esteem Him.
Surely our griefs He Himself bore,
And our sorrows He carried;
Yet we ourselves esteemed Him stricken,
Smitten of God, and afflicted.
But He was pierced through for our transgressions,
He was crushed for our iniquities;
The chastening for our well-being fell upon Him,
And by His scourging we are healed.
All of us like sheep have gone astray,
Each of us has turned to his own way;
*But the L*ORD *has caused the iniquity of us all*
To fall on Him.
He was oppressed and He was afflicted,
Yet He did not open His mouth;
Like a lamb that is led to slaughter,
And like a sheep that is silent before its shearers,
So He did not open His mouth.
By oppression and judgment He was taken away;
And as for His generation, who considered
That He was cut off out of the land of the living
For the transgression of my people,
To whom the stroke was due?
His grave was assigned with wicked men,
Yet He was with a rich man in His death,
Because He had done no violence,
Nor was there any deceit in His mouth.
*But the L*ORD *was pleased*
To crush Him, putting Him to grief;
If He would render Himself as a guilt offering,

He will see His offspring, He will prolong His days,
*And the good pleasure of the L*ORD
will prosper in His hand.
As a result of the anguish of His soul,
He will see it and be satisfied;
By His knowledge the Righteous One,
My Servant, will justify the many,
As He will bear their iniquities.
Therefore, I will allot Him a portion with the great,
And He will divide the booty with the strong;
Because He poured out Himself to death,
And was numbered with the transgressors;
Yet He Himself bore the sin of many,
And interceded for the transgressors."

Isaiah 53:1-12 NASB

After Ann read me that Scripture, my first comment was, "I know that Scripture was right out of the New Covenant." She laughed, telling me that it was actually in the Old Covenant, our precious Holy Scriptures. Then I recalled my days growing up in our conservative synagogue in Iowa, and remembered that our rabbi was questioned as to why he skipped that portion in the Torah readings. He told us that he was tired of explaining to his congregants that this passage was not referring to Jesus, but to Israel. Suddenly the veil was beginning to lift, and I saw plainly that this passage in Isaiah was indeed a clear picture of the suffering Messiah *Yeshua.*

Ann prayed again, and this time the Lord led her to a passage talking about the Jewish people in the New Covenant, Romans 11. There were two verses in that chapter that spoke directly to my heart. Romans 11:15 refers to the Jewish people's rejection of the Messiah:

"For if their rejection brought reconciliation to the world, what will their acceptance be but life from the dead?"

Romans 11:15

Romans 11:24 compares non-Jews to "wild" branches, and the Jewish people to the "natural branches":

"After all, if you were cut out of an olive tree that is wild by nature, and contrary to nature were grafted into a cultivated olive tree, how much more readily will these, the natural branches, be grafted into their own olive tree!"   Romans 11: 24

The rest of that chapter spoke to me as well. The veil was beginning to lift even more. *Yeshua* was giving me the ability to understand that even though for a time the Jewish people rejected Him, when they do begin to recognize that He is indeed their Messiah, it will be an amazingly joyful revelation!

After I left Ann, I told Dave about my experience with her. We had been invited to attend another prayer meeting and decided we would go. At that point we felt we had nothing to lose.

When we returned to the church, we were met with so much love that when one of the priests asked us if we wanted to ask *Yeshua*, Jesus, into our hearts, we both said in unison, "Yes!" Together we knelt down and were led in a simple prayer:

"Dear Yeshua, we recognize that You are the Messiah for the Jewish people, and for all of mankind. Please forgive us for our sins, and together we invite You into our lives and hearts to rule and reign for all eternity. We recognize that You suffered and died for us (Isaiah 53), and we thank You for Your great love. We completely dedicate our lives to serve You for as long as You have us on this earth. In Yeshua's name, Amen!"

Following that prayer, for the first time in my life, I began crying tears of joy. I felt like I was instantly being changed, and II Corinthians 5:17 became a reality:

"Therefore, if anyone is in Christ, the new creation has come: The old has gone, the new is here!"

II Corinthians 5:17

I had indeed become a new creation. I felt like I had been given a new lease on life. And yet my experience is not unique. I personally know hundreds of Messianic Jewish believers who have testified that they felt that they too had been given a new lease on life once they accepted *Yeshua* into their lives!

There is a Scripture that says the Jew requires a sign (I Cor 1:22), and what happened next was surely the sign that confirmed that my salvation was real. I was the only one in our family who did not have the opportunity to learn Hebrew or have a *Bat Mitzvah*. However, the moment I accepted *Yeshua* as my Messiah, I began speaking Hebrew. There was a nun present who understood Hebrew and translated what I was saying. She exclaimed that I was praising the Lord and thanking Him for revealing Himself to me as the long awaited Messiah!

After that, a man who was present at the prayer meeting had a special prophetic word for me, "Goldie, your gift will be the gift of joy." Immediately I felt a rush of joy! I intuitively recognized that it was a supernatural gift from the Lord, particularly special since I had been very depressed throughout most of my childhood. We all stood stunned and in awe, and our faith went up several notches!

Dave's experience of salvation was quiet, but very real and deep. Perhaps since we are so opposite in personalities, Dave as an introvert and me as an extrovert, our experiences were so very different. I believe that the Lord meets us each in a very personal way. Dave and I will forever treasure that special day, August 4, 1974. I was 25,

Dave was 23, and that evening we had both stepped into a loving and deeply profound relationship with *Yeshua*.

When I awoke the next morning, the colors were brighter and more vibrant. I never recall seeing the sky so blue, or the grass with such a deep green hue. I had so much joy that I could hardly contain myself! This was the first time I caught a glimpse of my rainbow, beginning to shine its brilliance into the night.

Dave and I had been living together, and we knew right away that the Lord was not pleased with that arrangement. We decided we would make plans to get married in the next couple of months.

Exploring Chapter 4

My Thoughts

It's interesting to note that even without the Lord, I knew that my affair with Sam was not right. But I did not have the courage to end it on my own. It is miraculous how the Lord intervened in my life and revealed the God-sized hole in my heart. The day that I fell on my face in the woods and cried out to Him with all my heart, I had faith that He would hear me! My life was forever changed; from that day forward I would never be the same.

Your Turn

Can you identify a crisis of faith in your life? What were the circumstances, and where did it lead you?

Chapter 5
Marrying My Soul Mate

"Though one may be overpowered,
two can defend themselves.
A cord of three strands is not quickly broken."

Ecclesiastes 4:12

*A*lthough I wanted my marriage to be a time of great joy and excitement, my parents did not take kindly to the idea that I had decided to marry someone outside of the Jewish faith. Thankfully, they didn't take drastic steps to disown me as they had done with my sister Esther. However, they did make it very clear that they were disappointed in my choice, not only because of our different faith, but also because his family background was so very dissimilar to ours. Dave came from a working class family, and no one in his family had attended college. Many in my family had professional careers and college degrees.

In those days, no rabbi would agree to marry a Jew and a non-Jew, so we asked a Justice of the Peace to marry us. Only my parents and one friend would be present at the ceremony as witnesses.

Our special day finally arrived, November 23, 1974! We made our way to St. Paul, Minnesota, where my father had located a Justice of the Peace. My father had relaxed somewhat by then, and in jest he said to us just before the ceremony, "Even though this only costs $10.00, it's not too late to change your mind. I haven't paid the Justice of the Peace yet. You have to remember this thing called marriage is easier to get into than it is to get out of!" Well, we certainly didn't take him up on his offer!

After the ceremony, my parents treated us to dinner at a beautiful hotel restaurant with a gorgeous panoramic view of the twin cities. My parents had given Dave and I an overnight stay at the hotel as a wedding gift. The following day, we flew to Connecticut to celebrate at an Italian restaurant with Dave's family, and then drove to Vermont for a short weekend honeymoon.

The pastor and our friends at our home church in Mankato held a wedding reception for us when we returned. It included a blessing ceremony and we recited our vows before the Lord. Ann, the hair stylist who led us to *Yeshua*, made me a beautiful wedding gown and styled my hair in a fancy up-do, and another friend made a wedding cake in the shape of a Bible. We had joined a worship band at our church, called "Free Spirit", and they played some moving worship songs during the ceremony and at the reception afterwards. After our vows, our pastor advised us to keep a "porcupine quill distance" between us. He cautioned us that if we are too close, we will hurt and smother each other, and if we are too far from one another, we will lose the intimacy between us. Those were compelling words that we have taken to heart throughout our many years of marriage.

I was offered a job in my field of Therapeutic Recreation in a psychiatric unit of a hospital in Minneapolis, so Dave and I moved again. Dave was still playing gigs with *The Honky Tonk Revival*. As a new believer in *Yeshua*, it was getting more burdensome for him to play in bars, since he felt that it was encouraging people to drink. One night as he was driving home after a gig, in a palpable way he felt the Lord telling him to quit the band and focus on his new found faith in the Lord.

When he told Sam that he was leaving the band, Sam became very angry and told Dave that he wanted nothing more to do with him. Leaving the band was a loss for Dave since he loved to perform, but in his heart he knew that it was the right thing to do and that it would be pleasing to the Lord.

At the same time the Lord convicted my heart, and I suddenly felt the weight of all the lies that I had told Dave in order to hide my affair with Sam. I decided to tell Dave the truth and to ask him to forgive me. Dave had always been somewhat suspicious that something was going on, but he had never confronted me.

I wasn't sure how Dave would react to the betrayal, and I was petrified to tell him. It took a lot of courage, but I knew that the Lord was convicting me. When I told him about the affair, since he had suspected that something had been going on between us, it was almost a relief for him to hear the truth. We both wept, and after we prayed together, Dave forgave me. However, it would take time for trust to build between us again. I would need to prove myself. As Dave saw that I was truly repentant and desired to remain faithful to him, trust was gradually restored. This is truly a testimony that the Lord lives in the center of our marriage, and this cord of three strands would not be easily broken!

Since accepting *Yeshua* as my Savior, I was in a quandary. How do I practice my faith as a Jewish person now believing in *Yeshua*? At that time, all the Jewish people I knew were still waiting for the Messiah's first appearance. I thought I was the only Jewish person in the world who believed that *Yeshua* is the Messiah.

We had not yet found a church home in Minneapolis. I tried going to a church, but it felt foreign and I didn't feel like I really belonged. One day I happened to go into a Christian bookstore and asked the sales person if she had ever met a Jewish person who believed in *Yeshua*. Much to my surprise, the sales clerk shared that she had recently met a Jewish believer and happened to have her phone number. I called her immediately and we connected right away.

This Jewish believer was originally from Brooklyn, New York, and had moved to Minnesota to attend college. A fellow student had introduced her to *Yeshua*, and she had accepted Him into her heart and life. She then met her non-Jewish husband at a Christian seminar. He had grown up in a small Minnesota town that was predominantly home to residents of Norwegian and Swedish descent, and had never met a Jewish person before. We also learned that like Dave and me, they were musicians, and we began talking about forming a Jewish Gospel group.

Still searching for a church to call home, we saw an advertisement in the paper that there was going to be a special meeting for anyone interested in helping to form a Messianic Jewish Congregation in the Twin Cities. The pastor who organized the meeting had been given a vision to lead a Messianic congregation. He was from Kansas, and had never met a Jewish person before.

All four of us attended the meeting, where we met several other Jewish people who had come to believe in *Yeshua*! This group of Messianic Jews began to meet on a regular basis, and in 1976 our fellowship became the Messianic Jewish Congregation of the Twin Cities. The four of us formed a worship band with a few other musicians, calling ourselves *Yeshua's Children*.

I loved my new job as the Director of Therapeutic Recreation at Fairview Community Hospital in Minneapolis. I was responsible for designing and implementing therapeutic activities for patients in both the locked and unlocked units.

I had learned a lot from my years volunteering at the state hospital where I grew up, and now I had the professional degree to enhance my experience. There were challenges along the way, and also a testing of my newfound faith.

One day while I was working in the locked unit, the only other staff member there needed to leave the unit for a while. She asked me to keep my eye on a female patient that had been known to attack other patients, but assured me that more than likely nothing would happen. Within minutes after the staff member left the unit, before I even knew what was happening, this patient knocked me to the ground and began pulling out my hair. I screamed and screamed and she eventually stopped. I was able to call for help and the staff member returned back to the unit and sedated the patient. Truthfully I was the one who could have used the sedation after that frightening experience!

I knew at that moment that I had a choice to make. I could walk away in fear, refuse to return to the locked unit, and never face that patient again, or, I could walk in faith and trust the Lord to give me grace and strength. I went home that night and asked Dave to join with me in prayer, believing that I would be able to face my fear in His strength, not my own.

The very next day I chose to go back on the locked unit and sit quietly next to the patient who attacked me. I knew that was necessary for my own peace of mind, but I also felt that she might sense my silent care and concern. She had retreated into her own world again and still had not yet uttered a word since her admission. Over the next few weeks, as the psychotropic medicine and therapy began to work, she slowly began getting better and eventually was allowed onto the open unit.

A few weeks after the incident, I was walking by the lounge when I heard someone calling out to me. I looked over and realized that it was the patient who had attacked me. I sat down next to her and she began speaking. She said she vaguely remembered physically hurting me and wanted to ask for my forgiveness. When I told her she was forgiven, she began to tell me her story. She admitted that she was a Type A personality, always on the go, and never took time to rest. Slowly, over time, she began experiencing stress and anxiety, which led to a nervous breakdown and a psychotic episode. She remembered very little about her experience in the locked unit, but with therapy and medicine, she began to realize that she needed to make drastic changes in her lifestyle. She kept in touch after she was discharged from the hospital, giving us regular progress reports on her successful lifestyle change.

This incident, along with several others I experienced while working on the mental health unit, led me on a quest to learn everything I could about stress. My own life was out of balance, and I wanted to make some lifestyle changes myself. I too was a Type A personality, and overweight, barely exercising and not caring about what I ate. As I began my research, I slowly started making changes and began to feel better and more balanced. I started taking classes to learn as much as I could about stress management, and eventually decided to form a corporation to help people cope with stress. I named my company *Caspian Associates* because people living close to the Caspian Sea are believed to be very healthy. Through *Caspian*, I designed noon hour stress relief programs, which I sold to major corporations such as 3M, Honeywell, and Blue Cross/Blue Shield. Since employees who participated in *Caspian* were more productive and required less sick leave, the companies considered the program very successful.

Another powerful experience in the locked unit involved a patient whom I will call "Fran". Fran was admitted to the locked unit with a history of psychotic episodes, depression, and a suicide attempt. Over time I learned that she loved music and had brought her guitar into the hospital. After the psychotropic medicines took effect, I requested that she be brought down to my clinic for private music therapy. She brought her guitar, and I asked her to play some songs she had written. Although she sang with much passion, the lyrics were very dark. The goal as a Recreation/Music Therapist is to start where the client is and bring her to a more positive place. I began slowly introducing her to music with more positive lyrics, and eventually she moved to songs that were more hopeful. Our sessions were very productive, and slowly the real Fran emerged. She was soon allowed onto the unlocked unit and could join all my music therapy sessions.

I had spoken to Fran many times about how the Lord had transformed me, and I was very hopeful that Fran would dedicate her life to the Lord and would be totally healed from mental illness. Before she was discharged, I obtained special permission to take her to my congregation for a service. My sister Esther, who also had become a Messianic Jew, was visiting the United States from Israel and was going to share her testimony that night. The worship and Esther's testimony touched Fran very deeply. Before she left, we prayed for a miraculous healing to take place in her life. Later that night, in the privacy of her hospital room, she gave her life to the Lord. The Lord indeed answered our prayer and completely healed Fran from mental illness. Her psychiatrist was astounded, for he had never witnessed complete healing from such a serious mental illness. Over the next several months, Fran was eventually able to stop taking all her psychotropic medicine.

As the years passed and Fran grew in her faith, she became a missionary and a worship leader in her church, and today she belongs to a deep intercessory healing prayer group. I recently received a letter from Fran, 42 years after her hospitalization. She thanked me for reaching out to her in the hospital and making a way for her to accept the Lord. Truly this was the greatest blessing that came from my job at Fairview Community Hospital. I am so grateful that the Lord used me as an instrument of His love and grace, and we remain "forever friends" to this day.

About this time, *Caspian Associates* was demanding much more of my time, so I resigned my position at Fairview Community Hospital. One of my clients at *Caspian* was a Messianic Jew and an author. She was overly involved in ministry and close to burnout, and had asked to meet with me for help with stress management.

After a few meetings, she quickly saw the value of making some healthy lifestyle changes. She asked if I would be interested in collaborating with her on a book to help others cope with stress. We procured a Christian publisher who gave us advanced royalties to begin writing. *Overcoming Stress: How to Establish a Balanced Lifestyle in an Unbalanced World*, by Jan Markell in collaboration with Jane Winn, was published by Victor Press in 1983.

From 1976 to 1983, Dave was working tuning and reconditioning pianos. Additionally, he worked part time with a commercial janitorial company. One day in the early 1980's, he got a call from the owner of the janitorial company. His manager had suddenly walked off the job, and the owner needed someone to step in. Impressed with Dave's work ethic, he asked Dave if he would manage the company. It was extremely good pay and would be great experience, so Dave accepted immediately. After one year's experience as manager, Dave began his own janitorial business. He was soon managing a number of commercial properties, and his owner-operated janitorial business became very successful.

Dave and I continued to serve in the worship ministry at the Messianic Jewish Congregation until the fall of 1983. During our tenure there, we met two people who soon became a significant part of our lives. Debbie was a Jewish woman who had come to believe in *Yeshua* and attended the discipleship class that Dave and I taught. She was a delightful and very talented young lady, and we were very impressed with how quickly she grew in her faith. David Chernoff was a man who was very involved in the Messianic Jewish Alliance of America and Congregation *Beth Yeshua* in Philadelphia. He would come to Minneapolis quite often to court Debbie, and eventually they were married.

Dave and I became very close to David and Debbie, and I began to sense that the Lord was leading us to move to Philadelphia and join their vibrant Messianic community. The adventure continues ...

"He brought me forth also into a broad place;
He rescued me because He delighted in me."
Psalm 18:19 NASB

Exploring Chapter 5

My Thoughts

I was given an amazing opportunity to come alongside Fran while she was still a patient in the locked unit, and to use music as a way to reach into her soul and give her purpose and hope.

Your Turn
    Was there a time in your life when you were given the opportunity to make a difference in someone else's life?

Chapter 6
Trusting an Unknown Future to a Known God

"He will be the sure foundation for your times,
a rich store of salvation and wisdom and knowledge;
the fear of the LORD is the key to this treasure."

Isaiah 33:6

Since my parents lived in Iowa, occasionally we would drive down from Minneapolis to visit them. We would make every effort to make the trip for the Jewish holidays. My parents did not yet know that I had accepted *Yeshua* into my life as my Lord and Savior. The conversation had never come up and, anticipating a very harsh reaction from my father, I certainly did not want to broach the subject.

In the spring of 1978, just before my parents retired and moved to Arizona, we made the trip down to Iowa to celebrate Passover with them. After the Seder, we retired to the den to watch television with my father. There was a show on which featured a rabbi, a priest, and a Protestant minister. Passover and Easter overlapped this year, and they were discussing their views regarding Jesus as the Messiah.

All of a sudden my father turned to me and said, "You don't believe in Jesus, do you?" Four years old in the Lord, I was totally caught off guard and suddenly stricken with fear. How do I answer this question? If I tell him the truth, will he disown me? Will he have a heart attack? On the other hand, I knew that I did not want to deny the Lord. I remembered what happened to the disciple Peter and how he was full of remorse after his denial of Jesus three times. For a moment I felt paralyzed by the fear of man and couldn't open my mouth. When he asked me again, I blurted out "Yes, Daddy, I do believe in Jesus."

At that point he began screaming, "You are no longer a Jew! You are just like Hitler, slowly annihilating the Jewish people by believing in Jesus! There is only one God. Hitler believed in Jesus! How are you different than him? I want you to know I love you less because of this, and when I tell your mother she will feel the same way!"

At that moment everything became a blur, and I remember bursting into tears and running out of the room, Dave in pursuit. Because it was so important for me to know that my father loved me, I was totally crushed and completely devastated. Dave tried consoling me, but the rejection was very deep. I could not cope with the knowledge that my father loved me less. Since there was so much tension, we decided to head back up to Minneapolis the next morning. I remember feeling numb the whole ride back, although Dave was trying very hard to comfort and pray for me.

This re-opened the old wound of rejection, and I began slipping back into depression. Dave suggested that I meet with a Christian counselor to help me process through the myriad of feelings.

A few days later, I received a vitriolic letter from my father reiterating what he had said in his rant, accusing me of acting just like Hitler. He also stated that my grandparents would be rolling over in their graves since I no longer believed in the God of Abraham, Isaac, and Jacob. I understood what my father meant. Many Jewish people who have not yet come to embrace *Yeshua* believe that *Yeshua* was a prophet who certainly did a lot of good when He walked on the earth, but they do not recognize His Deity.

My counselor helped me to sort out my feelings and to recognize that ultimately, I had to please the Lord and not my father. She suggested that I give him some space and begin praying for his heart to change. Over the next several months of counseling and prayer, I began to feel more hopeful and to grow in my relationship with the Lord. In many ways the attack from my father helped me to cling to the Lord, my trust in Him deepened, and my rainbow in the night shined brighter.

Later that year, just before my parents made the move to Arizona, we invited them to come to visit us in Minneapolis. We knew it would be more difficult to visit them once they moved to Arizona. By this time, my father had calmed down considerably, so we hoped that they would accept our invitation. We also took a huge risk and invited them to attend our Messianic congregation when they visited.

Much to our surprise and delight, they accepted our invitation to visit, and even agreed to attend our congregation! The Lord brought to mind the Scripture:

"He will turn the hearts of the parents to their children, and the hearts of the children to their parents."
Malachi 4:6

Since it was close to their wedding anniversary, we decided to surprise them with a reception. We wanted them to meet other Messianic Jews, and also to feel more comfortable when they came to our congregation, so we invited all our friends to the anniversary reception. My parents were very surprised and touched by the outpouring of love from our friends and from Dave and me as well. It definitely broke the ice before visiting our Messianic congregation. When they attended the service, they both appeared relaxed and shared that they enjoyed the experience. They commented on how much joy was present in the service. Their willingness to accept and love us even though we espoused a different belief system was a real turning point in our relationship. Over the next several years much healing took place, and we enjoyed an increasingly amicable and peaceful relationship with them.

Debbie and David Chernoff were married in October of 1983. Debbie had asked me to be in her wedding party, and Dave and I flew to Philadelphia. We had gotten to know and love more people from the Messianic community affiliated with Congregation *Beth Yeshua*. It was a vibrant community with over 300 people, who lived in close proximity to the Congregation. Dave and I were feeling that the Lord might be leading us to move to Philadelphia.

Dave was not as certain as I was, but we both agreed to pray for clear direction from the Lord. Dave, the practical one, made it very clear that he would need specific signs from the Lord in order for him to consider the move. The first sign that he desired was a job offer in my field of Therapeutic Recreation for $20,000. This would carry us over financially as he would begin to re-build his janitorial business in the new location. The second sign Dave was looking for was an affordable place for us to live.

Dave flew back to Minneapolis after the wedding to attend to his janitorial business, but I decided to stay an extra week and explore career opportunities in my field. Before I started my job search, I met with David Chernoff's parents, Marty and Yohanna Chernoff, the leaders of Congregation *Beth Yeshua*. I asked them to pray with me for the Lord's will and direction. After the prayer, Yohanna and Marty had a peace about Dave and me moving to Philadelphia, and Yohanna had a word from the Lord. She said that she felt we would be moving to Philadelphia on

Thanksgiving Day of that same year, and that we would be having the holiday dinner at their house! That sounded impossible since Thanksgiving was only a little over a month away. But, if a word is truly from the Lord, it will surely come to pass.

I began looking through the paper to see if there were any jobs available. At that time the salary for a Recreation Therapist was in the $14,000 range, so Dave's directive that I be offered $20,000 did not seem at all feasible. I found a job available in a psychiatric hospital about thirty minutes away from the Messianic community. I called and requested an interview as soon as possible since I would be leaving for Minneapolis in a week. They agreed, and when I came in for the interview, they asked if I could spend the entire day there so they could observe how I interacted with the staff and patients. At the end of the day, the Director asked to meet with me privately. She proceeded to tell me that the staff was very impressed with my skill set, and she offered me the position. She went on to say that the salary listed was $14,000, but because of my experience and expertise, they would like to offer me $20,000!

To say that I was in shock was an understatement. I told them that I was flattered, but that I would not be able to start until after Thanksgiving. She went on to say that she had already discussed it with the staff, and they all agreed to work overtime until I was able to relocate and assume the position. You can imagine Dave's shock when I called and told him the news!

The next big hurdle was finding a place to live. A friend from *Beth Yeshua* took me to a local realtor. The realtor took us to a row home in the heart of the Messianic community.

An elderly woman greeted us at the door. When I told her of our situation, and that we wouldn't be able to move in until December 1st, she answered, "I am Jewish and I will soon be moving to Florida. My husband died several years ago, but we lived in this house for over thirty years. I want to rent it to someone special, and I feel God sent you here. I am willing to hold it for you until December 1st, and you don't have to pay the security deposit or any rent until after you get settled."

We were flabbergasted. The realtor told us that in all of his years as a real estate agent, he had never seen anything like this take place. I accepted the kind offer, and couldn't wait to tell Dave that his second condition had been met! When Dave heard the news, he agreed that the Lord had made it clear that it was His will for us to move to Philadelphia.

After I arrived back in Minneapolis, things moved into high gear. In many ways, it was an extremely hard decision because we had become deeply bonded to so many dear people in the eleven years we had lived in Minnesota. Our friends were very sad when they heard the news, but they supported us when they understood that the Lord was leading us to move to Philadelphia.

The next challenge was financial. We needed quite a bit of money to pay for the move and to carry us over until we got settled in Philadelphia. It would also be a while before I actually received my first paycheck. We were truly on a faith journey, and the Lord began to make it very clear that He was going to provide everything that was needed. As we began to pray in faith, our growing trust in Him banished our fears.

> "Blessed is man who trusts in the LORD,
> And whose trust is the LORD.
> For he will be like a tree planted by the water,
> That extends its roots by a stream
> And will not fear when heat comes;
> But its leaves will be green,

And it will not be anxious in a year of drought
Nor cease to yield fruit."   Jeremiah 17:7-8 NASB

The first exciting way the Lord provided for us financially was through a weekend women's retreat where I was speaking on overcoming stress. There were around two hundred women present, and by the end of the weekend I had sold all the books I had with me! This was almost the entire amount of money needed for the move.

The rest of the money came in stages from friends who were prompted by the Lord to give us certain amounts as going away gifts. By moving day, the Lord had provided all the money necessary to cover the cost of the move, and enough to live on until my first paycheck came in. The Lord's provision was such an encouragement, and greatly boosted our faith. Because we saw the hand of the Lord so clearly, it helped to ease the sadness we felt about leaving all our friends in Minnesota.

I was 34 years old and on the brink of a new adventure. The moving van arrived, and we loaded up both our furniture and our car. We were scheduled to fly out of Minneapolis the day before Thanksgiving, on November 22, 1983. However, the snow fell hard all day; the airport closed and our flight was canceled. In the eleven years we lived in Minnesota, there were many snowstorms, but we had never experienced one that was big enough to close the airport!

We were able to get a flight out early the next morning – which was Thanksgiving Day, and also our wedding anniversary. Yohanna's word that we would be moving to Philadelphia on Thanksgiving Day and in time to have dinner with them did indeed come to pass!

We stayed with friends the first week until the moving van arrived and we could move into our rental house. Our relocation to Philadelphia was a rough transition, but the kindness and generosity of the people in the community eased the transition. We were invited over to many people's homes for dinners, which greatly helped stretch our money. We felt the hand of the Lord so clearly on our lives during that time.

Finally the day arrived when the moving van pulled up to our house. I was very grateful to know that the next day I would be receiving my first paycheck. But after everything was unloaded, I realized that there was no more money left to buy food for that day. I felt the Lord clearly tell me to walk by faith to the grocery store and there would be supernatural provision. The store was only a block away, so with a sense of wonder, I headed off.

When I got to the store, I found it teeming with people. The Lord directed me to a shopping cart. Right there on the handle was a $20 bill that nobody else had seen! It was enough for me to get groceries for our meal that day. Our hearts were filled with the knowledge that indeed our wonderful heavenly Father supplies our daily bread! We were filled with a greater appreciation for how the Lord provided daily manna for our ancestors when they left Egypt and lived in the desert for forty years.

"And my God will supply all your needs according to His riches in glory in Christ Jesus."
Philippians 4:19 NASB

My job as a Recreation Therapist at the psychiatric hospital was rewarding yet very challenging – and increasingly stressful. As a visionary, I brought lots of new ideas for program enhancement. But the recreational equipment was outdated, the budget was very low, and the support staff was not motivated to change.

Dave was building up his janitorial business in our new location. Since he had such excellent references from the companies that he worked for in Minnesota, he was quickly able to procure a commercial property account. Because he did such excellent work, the manager recommended him to another property manager, and gradually his business began to flourish as it had in Minneapolis.

To supplement our income, Dave had found several miscellaneous jobs, and I facilitated stress management seminars for some law firms and for a Christian counseling center. But because we needed a certain amount of monthly income, I could not quit my stressful job at the hospital until the Lord made it clear. Every day I prayed for the Lord's grace, and He provided. I also asked Him to lift His grace when He felt it was time for me to move on. One morning, I woke up and I felt the absence of His grace for the job. I took it as a sign that it was time to leave the hospital. In faith I gave my two-week notice, trusting that He would be my sure foundation, and that He had something even better for me.

I heard about a cardiologist in South Philly who was looking for someone to help his cardiac patients recover from triple and quadruple bypass surgery. He wanted someone to teach them stress management skills and to encourage them to adopt healthy lifestyle changes. I felt led to call the cardiologist and let him know I was interested in the position. A day after I gave my two-week notice at the hospital, the cardiologist called me back to offer me the position! The salary was great and I could start right after I ended my job at the hospital.

I loved working with the patients who were recovering from heart disease. I instructed them in proper nutrition, taught them how to cope with frustration and anger, and led them in group therapy to encourage them to begin communicating their feelings directly. Many of them, particularly the Italian men, only knew one way to express anger – and it certainly wasn't pretty! I taught them the art of relaxation and how to implement appropriate stress management skills. One of my endearing male patients said that he would always remember my calming voice instructing him to relax and communicate appropriately instead of picking up a couch and throwing it!

The job was a delightful experience, and when it ended in 1989, it was very disappointing for all of us. The funding for this program had run out, but the cardiologist was very pleased with the results. He said that all of the patients who participated in my program had shown dramatic improvement in their heart tests and blood work.

The next part of my journey would prove to be very challenging, as once again my trust in a loving heavenly Father would be further tested. I would need to remember how many times He had stepped in and intervened in my life ...

"I remembered my songs in the night."   Psalm 77:6

Exploring Chapter 6

My Thoughts

Admitting to my father that I believed in *Yeshua* was petrifying. I was paralyzed with fear that he would reject me. More than anything, I yearned for my father's love and acceptance. My challenge was to overcome the fear of man, and to learn to please the Lord first. I needed to place my relationship with my father into the Lord's hands.

Your Turn

Was there a time in your life when you knew you had to stand up to someone you loved, and face possible rejection? How did you handle it?

Chapter 7
My Hope is Lost

"I called on your name, LORD,
from the depths of the pit."　　　　Lamentations 3:55

My father's entire identity was wrapped up in his career as a successful psychiatrist and hospital administrator. After a twenty-year tenure at the state hospital, he retired in 1978. When he retired, he stopped taking care of himself. My mother encouraged him to pursue some of his past hobbies or consider serving as a consultant in his field, but to no avail.

My mother had been clear with my father that when he retired, she was going to pursue her dream to become a real estate agent. She followed through and eventually procured her license as a broker, and was doing well in her new career. But Dad resented it and did not like the role of "Mr. Mom". He became increasingly more depressed, and even though he had the warning sign of chest pain, he refused to see a cardiologist. Whenever he felt angina coming on, he popped some nitroglycerin. Overeating and lack of exercise also led to his deteriorating heart condition.

I visited them in Arizona a couple years after they retired. While walking one evening with my father, he told me that he felt very empty inside. He went on to say, "I'm a *nobody*. Not one person here knows me as Dr. Korson. No one knows all that I have accomplished in my career. All I have to show for it is our lovely house here in Arizona."

I tried reassuring him, "But Daddy, what really matters is not what you have accomplished in your life, but who you are as a person. You did so much good for the mentally ill and helped to remove the stigma of mental illness in that community. My hope is that you can hold that image of yourself in your heart and remember all the compassionate care you provided for so many in that hospital."

I could tell by the blank look on his face that my words fell on deaf ears. I left that visit heartbroken that my father could not even enjoy the retirement for which he had worked so hard. According to my mother, he continued to retreat into his own private world and would not seek treatment for depression or for the heart condition.

One morning in the summer of 1988, I received a call from my mother informing us that my father had been admitted to the hospital with a heart attack. She did not know how much longer he would live, so I made plans to fly down to Arizona as quickly as I could.

My younger sister Cathy was in New Mexico, and I was able to contact her to let her know about Dad's condition. It would be harder to contact my older sister, but the Lord took care of that. Esther was on a speaking tour in South Africa, encouraging people to obey God, to trust in His love for them, and to understand the place of Israel in His heart. She had felt from the Lord to call Mom, and so had learned the news. Because of the distance, it would take her a few days to reach Arizona.

I did not know if my father would even be alive by the time I arrived. While on the plane flying down to Arizona I was praying for him, and suddenly I felt the palpable presence of the Lord. I felt impressed to take out some paper to write what the Lord would say. I heard Him speak very clearly: *"When you arrive your father will be alive.*

Remember that your father loved the God of Abraham, Isaac, and Jacob. I will not allow him to perish until he **sees** *Yeshua as his Messiah."* After that word, a deep peace came over me. I knew that everything would be fine and that Dad would be alive when I arrived.

Mom's two sisters, Henrietta and Sandy, had arrived in Arizona and were there to comfort her. I walked into the hospital room and found Dad on oxygen and intravenous medications. When I was alone with him I prayed for him and held the word I had received from the Lord close to my heart.

After a few days, he began to feel better. It didn't appear as if he was at death's door any longer. My dad and I had some wonderful heartfelt conversations, made peace, and forgave each other for past hurts. Since Dad was improving and Esther would be arriving in a couple days, my mother encouraged me to fly back home to my husband in Philadelphia. Back at home, Dave and I and our friends from *Beth Yeshua* prayed for the Lord's will regarding my father.

Esther arrived in Arizona a couple days after I left, and then Dad took a turn for the worse. At 5:30 AM on the morning of August 26, 1988, the Lord woke me up out of a very deep sleep. I went downstairs and sat down at the kitchen table. I felt the strong sweet presence of the Lord come over me. I felt His prompting to close my eyes. As soon as my eyes closed, I saw a very clear vision of my dad in heaven. He was smiling and looked so peaceful, and appeared to be ageless. Two minutes later my mother called to inform me that he had just died a few minutes earlier. I was so grateful for that vision that prepared me for the news of his death. I held it in my heart, knowing that the word that I had received from the Lord on the plane most assuredly had come to pass.

Mom's sisters had already left Arizona, so Mom and Esther were there alone. Since there is no embalming in the Jewish religion, the burial would happen soon after death. Since my aunts and I had been able to see and talk with my dad when we were in Arizona, both my mom and Esther felt that it wouldn't make sense for all of us to fly down there again. They made the decision that the two of them would have a simple graveside service for Dad the next day. My special friends at *Beth Yeshua* held a beautiful memorial service for my father so that I could have closure.

A couple days after the burial, Mom called to talk with me. She mentioned that in the forty-eight years they were married, she had never seen such a look of peace on Dad's face as when he died. She said it was almost as though he saw something. This began her search for more answers. She asked to come visit us in Philadelphia to learn more about our beliefs.

We invited her to stay with us, and after her arrival she requested a meeting with Yohanna Chernoff and several other people from *Beth Yeshua*. She attended our Friday night *Shabbat* service, which she thoroughly enjoyed. Afterwards, Mom shared with us that she was struck by our fervency of belief, and how we chose liturgy that held special meaning for us. She explained that she was always taught never to believe that Jesus was the Messiah, but that she didn't just want to believe what she had been told all her life. She wanted to find out the truth for herself. She also began sharing about some hypocrisy that she had witnessed in the lives of some observant Jewish people in her family and in her neighborhood when she was a child growing up in Connecticut. She felt that many of them were judgmental and narrow-minded and were practicing their faith more out of obligation than from their hearts.

My mom left Philadelphia with hopeful expectation. Though she missed my father, she wanted to know more about the personal relationship with the Lord that she witnessed at *Beth Yeshua* and in our lives. When she

returned to Arizona, a Christian friend of hers helped her
to find a Messianic congregation near her home.

We received a call from Mom about six months
after her visit. It was June 12, 1989, the eve of my 40th
birthday. If Dave wasn't on the other line as a witness,
the conversation that followed would have been almost
impossible to believe.

With great excitement my mom exclaimed, "As you
know I have been doing much soul searching. After
visiting you and attending *Beth Yeshua* I have come to the
conclusion that *Yeshua* is the Messiah, and I would like for
you to pray the salvation prayer with me. Esther is coming
in from Israel tomorrow, and I would love to tell her when
she arrives that I too am now a Messianic Jew!"

After I recovered from the shocking news, we led her
in the prayer of salvation, and Mom happily told Esther
the news when she arrived in Arizona the next day. Mom
continued to grow in *Yeshua*, faithfully attending the
Messianic congregation near her home for many years.

The following fall for *Sukkot*, the Jewish Feast of
Tabernacles, I went to visit Esther in Israel. I shared with
her the prophecy that I had received from the Lord about
Dad while I was on my flight down to Arizona after his
heart attack. All of a sudden Esther began to cry. She told
me that while she was seated at his bedside, just before
he died, he had exclaimed, with real wonder in his voice,
"Wait until you **see** *Yeshua*!" My joyful tears joined hers
as we recognized that the prophecy had indeed come true!
What an amazing confirmation!

I also shared with her the vision that I had of Dad in
heaven on the morning he died. Esther and I had prayed
for my parents' salvation for so many years. There, in the
heart of Jerusalem, we rejoiced that our prayers had been

answered! What a joyous celebration indeed!

"With man this is impossible, but with God all things are possible." Matthew 19:26

When Dave and I had first met in 1971, we made a decision together not to have children. At that time, we both felt that because of our difficult childhoods, we would not be effective parents. However, I had a change of heart after we were living in Philadelphia. At *Beth Yeshua*, I saw many happy couples with children who seemed so fulfilled. By this time I was 40 years old, and my biological clock was ticking away. Almost overnight, or so it seemed, I woke up one day with an overwhelming desire to have a baby.

I was hopeful that all these years later Dave would have changed his mind also. But when I broached the subject, Dave made it clear that he had not changed his position and could not see himself as a father. No matter how much I tried to convince him that we would be wonderful parents, he was adamant that it could not work for him. He did not want to risk emotionally damaging a child the way that he was damaged in his own childhood.

My job with the cardiologist had ended and I had not yet found another job. The lack of productive work coupled with my unfulfilled desire for children caused me to slip back into depression. I had very little sense of worth and felt like my life was devoid of meaning or purpose.

I located a therapist who, like me, initially did not want to have children but then later changed her mind. Dave agreed to meet with her. My hope was that after Dave worked through his feelings with this therapist that he too would have a change of heart. Dave spent a year in therapy with her, and it became apparent that Dave was still unable to see himself as a father. I was doing everything I could to convince Dave that we needed to have a baby. It was not working, and this issue was ripping our marriage apart. We were fighting and began to drift further and further apart.

One morning, as I was having my devotional time with the Lord, I once more felt His familiar presence in a palpable way. I heard Him say to me that there was going to be a season where the gift of joy would be lifted so that I could learn to trust Him in a deeper way. He assured me that we would walk closely together through this dark stage of my journey. He promised that at the end of the season, when He restored the gift of joy, that my inner and outer joy would be married together. I entered my "dark night of the soul". Yet I knew that I must put my trust in Him, for He Himself had given me His assurance that His joy would come in the morning.

"For His anger is but for a moment,
His favor is for a lifetime;
Weeping may last for the night,
But a shout of joy comes in the morning."
Psalm 30:5 NASB

I can still remember the moment the joy left me. Feeling empty and full of despair, I had lost hope and could see no rainbow in the darkness. I did not have a career, I was not going to be a mom, and my husband and I were drifting apart. That night I actually wanted to die. I phoned my very dear friend Rhona, who is a professional counselor, and told her how I was feeling. She listened with compassion, but challenged me to seek the Lord and cling to Him. She prayed a beautiful prayer for me, and I felt a glimmer of hope. I was not actively suicidal and did not have a plan to take my life, but as the days and weeks passed by, I had no motivation whatsoever. I could not even look for another job, and for hours on end I would just lie on the couch and feel sorry for myself.

Unlike the friends of Job of the Bible, my friends during this season were amazing. Debbie would invite me to take morning walks, and she always prayed for me. My friend Mindy, who owned horses and knew how much I loved them, would often show up at my house unannounced. She knew that I was depressed, and offered to take me out into nature. Many times she drove me to the barn where her horses were boarded. She would take me on beautiful trail rides in the woods. During those rides I would feel alive again and hopeful that one day I would have a sense of purpose in my life. But as soon as Mindy dropped me off at home, I would fall back into depression and despair.

I could see the toll my depression was taking on Dave's life. His face was lined with worry and concern, but he felt helpless because he could see no way out of this dilemma.

One morning, Debbie had an epiphany while we were walking together. After praying for me, she had a strong sense from the Lord that perhaps it might not be the Lord's will after all that we have children. She reminded me that Dave had sought professional help and received much prayer about this issue. It was apparent that nothing had changed in Dave's heart. He had been willing to pursue the counseling and was open to a heart change, but it never happened.

I did not want to admit that Debbie may be right, because I had my heart set on having a baby. After our walk that day, I sat down to spend some time with the Lord. I felt His still small voice telling me that if I continued to press Dave to have a baby, over time, Dave might give in. But did I really want to take matters into my own hands, much like Sarah did with Hagar? This was a very sobering thought.

That night I sat outside on our patio. We had an open

awning and a clear view to the sky. Without warning, I felt overtaken by wrenching sobbing. It was more like wailing for my lost child. I felt so alone and helpless. I believed that surely the Lord had forgotten me – much like Sarah must have felt when she could not get pregnant with Abraham. Then suddenly, I felt a deep blanket of peace come over me and I stopped sobbing. I heard the still small voice of my Lord speak again to me in the darkness of night: *"My daughter, look up and see all the stars in the sky. Do you know I love you more than all those stars?"*

With trepidation I whispered, "Yes Lord."

He went on to say, *"In heaven, it won't matter if you don't have a baby on this earth. You need to keep an eternal perspective. I have a plan for your life, and you need to trust me to fulfill it. What does matter is how you respond to your husband, and that you totally surrender your desire to have a baby. You need to trust that I will never leave you nor forsake you."*

This is the Scripture that came to mind after this heartfelt conversation:

"I know the plans I have for you," declares the Lord,*"plans to prosper you and not to harm you, plans to give you hope and a future."*   Jeremiah 29:11

I knew with my whole heart that the Lord had spoken to me. I sat there for a long time pondering His words in my heart. Although I was filled with sorrow, I knew what I needed to do. I cried out to the Lord for mercy and begged Him to heal my broken heart.

"The Lord *is close to the broken hearted and saves those who are crushed in spirit."*   Psalm 34:18

With all the courage that I could muster, through grief-stricken tears, from the depths of the pit I totally surrendered to the Lord my desire to have a baby. I trusted Him to redeem my sinful behavior and bring beauty from the ashes. Afterwards, I felt His loving presence, and I imagined that He was holding me on His lap. He was reassuring me that He loved me and was pleased that I could trust Him with the deepest desire of my heart.

Intuitively I knew that I needed to take an active step of faith to solidify the sacrifice that I had made to the Lord. I went inside and saw my husband sitting in the dark with his head in his hands. I could sense his pain. I knew in my heart of hearts how very much he loved me and never wanted to hurt me. I also recognized that he did not feel that he had the grace to take on the challenge of fatherhood. I knew that I needed to release him from this burden. My mother had recently commented that many couples needed to have children in order to define them. She went on to say that Dave and I did not need children, but that we were a complete couple without them.

I went over and sat next to Dave on the couch. I told him about my experience with the Lord, and that I wanted to release him from the burden of fatherhood. His reaction was indicative of his amazing character and love for me. He held me in his arms and we wept together for hours. He knew what a painful sacrifice this was for me. Likewise, I knew how hard it would have been for him to take on the enormous and overwhelming task of fatherhood because of his broken past.

After that conversation, I had more peace, but continued to grieve the loss of motherhood. Dave and I decided that it was important to tell David and Debbie Chernoff that we had made the decision that we would not be having children. We also wanted them to pray for us. The following Friday night we went to the *Shabbat* service at *Beth Yeshua.* Afterwards, we asked if we could speak to them.

We told our dear friends what we had decided, and through tears they prayed for us. They knew the enormity of the decision and wanted to make sure we knew that they were there to support us in any way they could. After the prayer David Chernoff had a word for me. "Goldie, the Lord knows your hurt and loss. But He wants you to know that one day you will be a mother to many." I had no idea what that meant, but I sensed a glimmer of a rainbow piercing this dark night. I hid those words in my heart, trusting that if the Lord inspired them, this prophecy would come to pass.

Slowly, I began to feel motivated to begin looking for a job. My friend Rhona had recently started working as a group therapist at Mirmont Addiction Treatment Center, which was not far from our home. She had heard that there was a position open for a Recreation Therapist, and suggested that I meet with the Clinical Director. I was feeling ready to begin working again, and the thought of working in the field of addictions was intriguing to me.

I followed up and had a productive interview with the Clinical Director. A few days later I was offered the position. I would be working with a Music Therapist who would be my immediate supervisor. I began my new position at Mirmont in April of 1989. This next stage of my journey would bring new revelation as I walked with the Lord, trusting Him to heal my broken heart day by day.

"Though I have fallen, I will rise.
*Though I sit in darkness, the L*ord *will be my light."*
Micah 7:8

Exploring Chapter 7

My Thoughts

Dave and I had to face one of the most difficult decisions any couple could face. There was such a miraculous transformation in my life after my surrender. The Lord's words gave me renewed hope and a sense of deep peace.

We can't define our lives by whether one door is better than another. Instead, we must focus on the fact that He always has a plan for our lives, which He will reveal in His perfect timing.

Your Turn

Can you identify with my heart wrenching decision to surrender to the Lord my deepest desire?

What is the Lord calling you to surrender right now?

Chapter 8
Restoration of Joy

"Now may the God of hope fill you with all joy and peace in believing, so that you will abound in hope by the power of the Holy Spirit." Romans 15:13 NASB

One morning, a few days before I was going to start my new job at Mirmont Addiction Treatment Center, I sensed the sweet presence of the Holy Spirit as I was having my morning quiet time. I heard His gentle whisper in my heart.

"My precious one, today I want you to receive back from Me your gift of joy in all its fullness. Together we walked through the valley of the shadow of death. You trusted Me with your deepest heart's desire, and placed it on the altar. I am well pleased. I am healing your broken heart, and now as your inner and outer joy match, you will experience a deeper intimacy with Me than you have ever known before. I will greatly use you to comfort others with the comfort you have received. I will redeem every shed tear for My glory. As you seek My face daily, I will lead and guide you every step of the way. Do not fear or be dismayed. I will walk closely by your side as you trust Me for further revelation in your story of redemption."

I basked in the Lord's loving presence as I savored every word. I felt as though the joy had been injected back into my spirit, and hope no longer eluded me. Everything looked brighter, and the wall of despair and sadness lifted. My heart was still tender. But after this divine encounter, I knew that He would redeem my pain by bringing forth purpose from it. I knew that I would be fully restored, and that one day I would see the bigger picture.

Dave and I were both involved with the music ministry at *Beth Yeshua*. We were also surrounded and cared for by our friends in this loving community. The brokenness in our marriage was beginning to heal, and the *"cord of three strands"* (Eccl 4:12) was strengthened as we both acknowledged that the Lord was indeed at the center of our marriage. This difficult journey brought us closer together as a couple and enabled us to serve Him in an even greater way.

I loved my new job at Mirmont. There were challenges, but working in the field of addiction was very rewarding. In the beginning, I worked closely with the Music Therapist for training purposes. Eventually, I led Therapeutic Recreation groups for adolescents and adults, and presented lectures encouraging a healthy lifestyle in sobriety.

A few months into my new job, I requested permission to observe one of the therapists who facilitated group therapy sessions for the female adolescents. I had no idea what to expect. As soon as we entered the room, she turned the lights down low and closed the blinds. She asked the participants to share a secret they had never revealed before. She reminded them that they are "only as sick as their secrets". She emphasized the need to open up and begin to trust others in this safe place. Otherwise, she warned, the possibility of relapse after discharge would be more probable.

As the session progressed, the young ladies began sharing some of their deepest hurts. One girl began to share about abuse at the hands of her father. She began crying, and without warning I began sobbing uncontrollably. Obviously this caught everyone by surprise and the therapist asked me to please leave the room and to wait in the next room for the group to end. When the group ended, the therapist told me that we were going to meet with my supervisor and the Clinical Director. I was still somewhat in shock that I was unable to keep my composure and had had an emotional outburst, especially since I was on staff.

When we arrived in the Clinical Director's office, the therapist proceeded to tell them what had transpired in the group. I blurted out, "That poor girl. I can't believe how much she has suffered." I was surprised to find myself crying again.

With compassion, the Clinical Director replied, "It's not about her. It's about you. When that young lady shared her story, it obviously triggered something in your life. I think it is very important that you get some professional help. There are probably family of origin issues that you need to address and work through so that you can close that chapter of your life." The Director recommended that I attend Caron Foundation's five-day intensive in-patient treatment program for co-dependency, which focused on family of origin issues. He wanted me to gain insight into my maladaptive coping responses so that I would be better equipped to help others heal from past hurts. He gave me a paid leave of absence to attend, explaining, "We see you as a valuable employee and want to see you identify and work through these issues so that you can live in the present and enjoy a productive life."

I certainly did not expect to hear that it was all about my issues! It took me a while to process this information, but once I accepted the situation, I thanked the Director and said that I would look into the program.

At home that night, I told Dave what had transpired, and he gave me his full support to pursue the Caron program. My health insurance paid for most of the costs under my mental health benefits, and Mirmont would pay my salary for that week. The first step was to participate in a phone intake, and then I would be admitted to the next available program. Caron Foundation, housed in a former Catholic retreat center, was located about fifty miles away.

Once my date of admission was procured, I made plans to drive to the treatment center. I did not know what to expect, and made sure that I had plenty of prayer support. The drive was beautiful, and when I arrived I was struck by the serene and idyllic setting. The grounds were gorgeous, and the treatment center was situated at the top of a very steep hill.

I was told that the other participants were also therapists, and that I would have a roommate. I was admitted by one of the therapists who would be co-facilitating our group. We were told that in order to stay focused on the program and immersed in our recovery process, we could not have any contact with the outside world during the five days. There were no cell phones back then, so I was not even tempted to call my husband or friends.

Those five days were incredible and life changing. Each morning and afternoon, we had two hours of very intense experiential therapy sessions with skilled and compassionate therapists. Part of our recovery required us to get in touch with our "inner child" that we had lost touch with somewhere along the way, so the therapy sessions were followed by childhood games. Throughout the week we also became the parents and siblings for each other, taking turns acting in the staging of each other's family of origin scripts. Each one of us had the opportunity to say what we had never been allowed to say in our families. It was very cathartic to express emotions that were once unacceptable. In essence, we reclaimed our power. As a group, we bonded in a very deep way. We wept, laughed, hugged, and celebrated each other's successes.

For me, the experience went very deep. I was finally able to come out of denial and get in touch with the reality of my family. I had always idealized my family, especially my father. When I had to face my "parents" in the role play, initially I regressed back to the helpless little girl. But eventually, with encouragement from the therapists and other group members, I found my voice and faced my fears. Since anger was never allowed in my family, it was extremely liberating to shout and yell what had been locked up inside me for so many years. It felt so real. When the anger subsided, everyone surrounded me in a huge group hug as I wept uncontrollably.

On our final night, the staff held a birthday party to celebrate and embrace our "inner child". It was a joyous occasion for all of us. We emerged from the week with a wonderful glow, looking several years younger.

On our last morning, we were told to meet in the chapel, which held stations of the cross. At each station there were many teddy bears and wonderful affirmations. Since we had received very little positive affirmation in our families of origin, this was very healing. I wept my way around all of the stations, and afterwards I bought a tiny teddy bear in their gift shop to remind me to always care for my "inner child". I still have the teddy bear to this day!

Before discharge, we met individually with one of our therapists to set up a care plan based on the issues that were addressed throughout the week. My therapist strongly encouraged me to pursue therapy and to attend a Twelve-Step Program in order to continue working on my co-dependency issues. When we all met together for the final closing ceremony, we shared what we would be taking home from the program. It was astounding to hear each other's stories, and the change on each one's face was visible.

When I arrived home, Dave and all of our friends could see the difference in my countenance. I truly experienced the reality of the Scripture, *"Then you will know the truth, and the truth will set you free"* (Jn 8:32). I was so grateful for the staff at Mirmont who had made it possible for me to attend this life-changing program. I received so much healing as I gained insight into my maladaptive coping responses, and I came out of the program better equipped to help others heal from past hurts.

My job became a lot easier with the new self-confidence and insight into my propensity for co-dependency. One of the slogans at the treatment center applied to my recovery: *With awareness you can change.*

Every day at work was a new adventure, and the therapy and Twelve-Step support groups I was now attending helped me to navigate my life with new positive coping strategies. But there would soon be another unexpected turn in the road that would test my newfound identity and confidence.

Exploring Chapter 8

My Thoughts

I did not expect to lose control in the group therapy session at the rehab, but the Lord knew all along that it was time for me to face some of my family of origin issues.

"And we know that God causes all things to work together for the good of those who love God, to those who are called according to His purpose."   Romans 8:28

That experience opened the door for me to attend the Caron Foundation five-day program for co-dependency issues.

Your Turn

Have you experienced a time in your life when circumstances triggered an unexpected flood of emotions? Could there be deep-seated issues that the Lord is exposing and inviting you to address?

Chapter 9
My Hidden Treasure

"I will give you hidden treasures,
riches stored in secret places,
so that you may know that I am the Lord,
the God of Israel, who summons you by name."

Isaiah 45:3

After my in-patient experience in the treatment center for co-dependency, I continued to grow in my self-confidence in my job at Mirmont. I was not so easily thrown off emotionally when I had a difficult group, and I became more assertive with my clients. I truly loved this job and enjoyed working in the field of addiction. I was completely unprepared when, only a year into the job, I once again was called into the Clinical Director's office.

The Clinical Director told me that insurance companies were no longer paying for adjunctive therapies such as Therapeutic Recreation. This was my two-week notice that my position had been terminated. To say that I was in shock was truly an understatement. I felt as if the wind had been knocked out of me, and I promptly excused myself. I was given permission to leave early that day, and I drove right over to see Dave at work. As soon as I saw him I burst into tears. He scooped me up into his arms as I told him what had transpired. He immediately prayed for me, and assured me that the Lord would take care of us.

He insisted that we needed to trust Him.

The Lord had already prepared a prayer meeting at *Beth Yeshua* that night, and I sensed that He wanted me to attend. I felt numb and was not yet ready to share with anyone about the job loss. I walked in quietly. David Chernoff immediately had a word that someone in the room was feeling despair, and he prayed for whoever that person might be. I knew that the word was meant for me, but I did not say anything. As I was leaving, David stopped me and asked if I was that person. I admitted that I was, and he prayed a beautiful prayer, assuring me that the Lord had His hand on my life and that He had a perfect plan. I felt a little more peace as I left that night.

Over the next two weeks, thoughts of hopelessness continually swirled around in my mind. I had to repeatedly ask the Lord for strength and peace so that I would not fall back into despair. Once again, I suddenly felt that I had no identity. I wasn't going to be a mother, and now I no longer had a career. I felt darkness closing in, and once again I could not see God's rainbow.

I took a walk with a friend who had a degree in social work. She asked if I had ever considered going back to school to pursue a graduate degree, and strongly suggested that I consider pursuing the field of social work. She explained that the other mental health fields required many hours of counseling and supervision after graduation before the licensing exam could be taken, but social work allowed graduates to sit for the licensing exam immediately after graduating. As she spoke, I felt the gentle nudging of the Holy Spirit that perhaps she was onto something. When Dave came home later that day I ran the idea by him. He didn't hesitate, and encouraged me to move forward. He assured me that because the janitorial business was going well, we were in a position to afford this.

I began researching the programs in the area, and found a graduate program at Bryn Mawr College, which was in close proximity to our home. Considered an Ivy League school, Bryn Mawr had an excellent reputation and its own distinctive degree. Since returning to school was such a big step, I decided that I wanted to pursue the best possible program in the field of social work. I prayerfully determined that this was going to be the only program I would consider.

With hopeful expectation mingled with a tinge of apprehension, I began the long and arduous task of completing the application process. When I was finished, I personally dropped off the completed application at the post office, praying for the Lord's will. Prospective students were told that Bryn Mawr College is very selective in their acceptance process, and that although 300 had applied, only 100 students would be accepted into the program. The waiting time would be thirty to sixty days before we would know whether or not we were chosen.

During that long period of waiting, I received an unexpected call from the Clinical Director at Mirmont requesting that I come in and meet with him. I had no idea what to expect, but agreed to come in.

I was delighted when the Clinical Director asked if I would be interested in working as a consultant at Mirmont for a few hours a week. The job entailed training the psychiatric technicians to facilitate groups focused on healthy lifestyle change. Not only would this be extra income while I was in graduate school, but healthy lifestyles was my area of expertise. I gladly accepted, and began to feel hopefully optimistic about my future. Mirmont offered me an excellent salary, which would certainly help with the cost of books and other expenses if I was accepted into the graduate social work program.

A month later, I received an envelope from Bryn Mawr College. I was so nervous that I asked Dave to open it. He read the words, "We are pleased to welcome you into the Bryn Mawr Graduate School of Social Work Program commencing in the fall of 1991 ending with graduation in May of 1993." I was shocked! In my heart of hearts I really didn't think I would be chosen from among so many applicants, especially since it was twenty years since I had completed my undergraduate degree. When it finally sank in that I was indeed accepted, I cried tears of joy and began calling family and friends to tell them the good news. As I held the acceptance letter in my hand, I could clearly see God's hand on my life.

That summer I began organizing and making preparations so that I would be ready to begin the very intensive course of study in the fall. There would be many books to read and papers to write. I knew it would require my full concentration, especially since I was 42 years old and had been out of school for so long.

Finally, opening day arrived. Like a child on the first day of school, I felt giddy and scared at the same time. The President of Bryn Mawr College gave the opening invocation, and the Dean of Social Work welcomed us, "You may feel like an imposter, but you were carefully chosen for this program. The whole faculty is committed to your successful experience and wants each of you to achieve a passing grade. However, if you are having difficulty with any of the classes or professors, it is your responsibility to communicate with them so they can help to resolve your issue." That definitely helped to alleviate some of the anxiety in the room, and we all breathed a collective sigh of relief. I was also relieved to know that the grading system was pass/fail and not letter grades.

With a sense of excitement and wonder, I entered the first day of classes. I felt the Lord's wonderful presence in that initial class. He was reassuring me that this was *my* "hidden treasure" that *He* had stored in secret places for such a time as this. He encouraged me not to see graduate school as His *second choice* for my life or as a *replacement* for not having children, but rather as part of *His bigger plan* for my life. He had revealed to me that He wanted me to help and encourage others with the comfort that I had been given from Him:

"... who comforts us in all our troubles, so that we can comfort those in any trouble with the comfort we ourselves receive from God."   II Corinthians 1:4

I began to deeply comprehend what He meant by redemption. He was promising to miraculously bring treasures and purpose *out of my failures.* A new day had begun, and I now had a renewed sense of purpose and could once again see His rainbow in the night. I had not been forgotten, and with that revelation, the despair lifted away and was replaced with a deep peace, joy, and hope for the future.

Exploring Chapter 9

My Thoughts

When I lost my job at Mirmont, I felt like I had once again lost my identity. I was not going to be a mother, and now I had no career. But in essence it was another opportunity for the Lord to redirect the course of my life according to His master plan.

Your Turn

Was there a "hidden treasure" revealed in your life after a loss or disappointment? Have you come to recognize that it is indeed a treasure, and not simply God's "second best choice" for you?

Chapter 10
Rivers in the Desert

"Behold, I will do something new,
Now it will spring forth;
Will you not be aware of it?
I will even make a roadway in the wilderness,
Rivers in the desert."   Isaiah 43:19 NASB

G raduate school was a shock to my system. I was not prepared for such computerization – even the card catalogue was totally absent from the library! I had not grown up with computers, and I found it very overwhelming. The school was aware that there were many older students unfamiliar with technology, so they scheduled a special class to acclimate us to the computerized library system.

It also took me a while to get used to the rigorous academic demands, which included writing many papers, preparing class presentations, and reading nearly a textbook each week. And I was definitely unprepared for the liberal environment on campus. Conservative values were frowned upon. I made a conscious decision during my first year of graduate school that before revealing where I stood with regard to my faith and political views, I would just focus on my studies and observe. I wanted the professors and my classmates to get to know me as a person before I took a stand that might be considered divisive.

Adding to the challenging course work was my part time job as a consultant at Mirmont. The consulting work was going very well, and I was pleased to remain in the field of addiction. Additionally, I realized that I was still mourning the loss of motherhood. I needed to allow for the emotional energy required to continue moving through the various stages of the grieving process.

Every morning during my quiet time with the Lord I prayed for strength and wisdom. I practiced my life Scripture every day:

"But seek first His kingdom and His righteousness, and all these things will be added to you."
Matthew 6:33 NASB

I knew that the key was living one day at a time, not looking ahead to all the work that would need to be completed by the end of each semester. I recognize that I could not have made it through that first year without the support and encouragement from my dear husband and the many prayers that were said on my behalf by my friends at Congregation *Beth Yeshua*.

The months flew by, and before I knew it I had completed my first year of graduate school. The end of the semester was a huge relief, and I was very grateful that I had the summer to recuperate before the final push.

The second year of graduate school required that we choose an internship to practice our clinical skills to complement our course work. I realized that I needed to assert myself in order to request that I be placed in a faith-based counseling internship. I soon discovered that there were no faith-based placements in their database. I had no choice but to request that the school consider adding one, and began to pray for the Lord to show me which one.

A friend of mine was on the Board of Directors at a faith-based center, Renewal Counseling. When I met with Bryn Mawr's Director of Placement, she was very gracious and allowed me to submit this agency for their approval. My request was accepted, and Renewal Counseling became the first Christian internship site at Bryn Mawr College! I knew that it was time for me to talk about my values in class when the opportunity presented itself.

One of my first challenges occurred when I wrote a paper identifying my role as a social worker as a life calling. The professor respectively disagreed with me, stating his belief that social work is a career and not a calling. However, as the semester progressed and he read more of my papers, he finally admitted that, indeed for me, it is a life passion and a calling.

One day in my Clinical class, a student stated that she had a Christian client and didn't know how to counsel her. I knew this was my opportunity to come forward and offer to help. I told the class that I was a person of faith, and that this was the population I would be working with as a social worker. The professor then asked if I would instruct the class that day and explain how to counsel someone with a faith-based background. She also requested that I talk about the unique issues that would need to be explored in the counseling process with those clients. I counted it as an honor, and gladly shared my expertise with the class.

I still laugh when one of the students, who had previously admitted that she was a lesbian, commented, "Well, now *you* have come out of the closet!" It was a wonderful moment of levity, and I had a sense of what it felt like to live as a minority where I was very different from the majority culture on campus. It reminded me of my high school days as a minority because of my Jewish heritage.

After that experience, I felt accepted by both students

and professors. My professors often asked my advice when students needed help with Christian clients. That sparked a seed in my heart, and I began to think about how the field of social work is designed to serve clients of every background. Yet Bryn Mawr had nothing in the curriculum to address people of faith. I decided to take a risk and approach the Dean of the Graduate School of Social Work. I told her point blank that Bryn Mawr College was far too liberal. I asked if it was really acceptable to leave out a large population of clients who espouse conservative values. She listened intently, and to my amazement agreed with me. She admitted that this issue had never been raised before, and perhaps now was a good time to take a closer look. Then she asked if I would consider presenting an all day workshop for social workers to better understand faith issues and the need to address this with their clients. They would be given continuing education credits to attend the workshop. I gladly accepted the challenge, and saw this as a ground-breaking opportunity to make a huge difference in the delivery of care for clients who want to integrate their faith into the counseling process.

I felt that the Holy Spirit was bringing rivers of life to the desert of faith in this community. I recalled my father's amazing legacy, and how the changes he made in a highly institutionalized system of mental health care paved the way for more humane treatment of the mentally challenged members of our society. Perhaps in my own way I was continuing his legacy, making a difference in whatever way I could in my sphere of influence. It was indeed a holy moment.

Exploring Chapter 10

My Thoughts

I needed to make a decision to move forward with my plan to attend graduate school. In a very real sense, I was moving to the acceptance stage in my grieving process.

Your Turn

Have you had to grieve the loss of a dream? What did God orchestrate in your life to help you move to acceptance?

Chapter 11
The Lord Takes Delight in Me

"The LORD your God in your midst,
The Mighty One, will save;
He will rejoice over you with gladness,
He will quiet you with His love,
He will rejoice over you with singing."
                                    Zephaniah 3:17 NKJV

he push was on as I entered into high gear for my final year of graduate school. I loved my internship, and it was such a joy to come alongside clients who wished to integrate their faith into the counseling process. The Director of Continuing Education had followed through and had approached the Social Work faculty at Bryn Mawr, recommending that I present an all day workshop focused on integrating faith and social work. Graduate students, faculty, and social workers in the field were welcome to attend and would be granted continuing education credit.

Initially, the idea was met with much resistance by the Bryn Mawr faculty. When pressed further, it became clear that this discussion was forcing them to revisit issues about their own faith, which many of them had abandoned years ago. It took quite a while to convince them, but the Director of Continuing Education asserted that if they were feeling threatened, this was all the more reason to bring this issue out into the open. These issues could be addressed in an honest and straightforward forum in a safe environment. Social workers could explore their own ambivalence about faith as it pertains to them personally, and then be in a position to help their clients. Finally, with much reservation, the faculty agreed to support the workshop on faith and social work.

This battle served to further convince me that the vision to integrate faith and social work in the graduate school curriculum was even more important than ever. I asked my supervisor at my internship site to co-facilitate this workshop with me. She was a seasoned social worker with many years of experience working in a Christian counseling center. She agreed to help me plan the outline for the seminar and to co-facilitate with me. It was exciting and daunting all at the same time.

During my last semester, it suddenly occurred too me that since Dave and I would not be having children, there would not be any *Bat* or *Bar Mitzvahs*, so we would need to find ways to bring family together for special occasions. I knew in my heart that my mom and some of our other relatives were aging, and we did not know how much longer they would be with us on this earth. I spoke to Dave about celebrating my graduation from Bryn Mawr by inviting family and friends to attend the ceremony with a reception afterwards. He agreed it was a wonderful idea, so I proceeded to let family and friends know. I realized that I was finally moving out of the grieving process and allowing myself to celebrate this critical milestone in my life.

David Chernoff at *Beth Yeshua* graciously offered to let us use the sanctuary for the reception, and our dear friend Caren agreed to help us with the music. Even though Caren was weak and terminally ill with metastatic breast cancer, she insisted on helping us. It was such a loving sacrifice and blessed us greatly.

My mother had recently been diagnosed with leukemia;

nevertheless, she would be flying in from Arizona. To my amazement, aunts, uncles, cousins, and even my sister Cathy and her young son Danny from California all gladly accepted our invitation. My older sister Esther was living in Israel, and I knew it would not be possible for her to attend, but her youngest son Mike would fly in from New York. My friends told me they would help me coordinate the event since they knew I would be busy finishing my studies. There were many demands on my schedule to complete all the required course work and internship hours, and the excitement of the upcoming family reunion helped me to get through the last semester.

As time was approaching for my graduation, I felt a sense of awe as I reflected on all that the Lord had done in my life since Dave and I made the decision not to have children. With His help, I had become better, not bitter. His redemptive hand was at work in my life, and even though things turned out very differently than I had originally desired, I was at peace. The Lord definitely had a plan for my life. I knew that He would use all of my life experiences for His glory, and to help others find hope and encouragement from my life story. From this vantage point, as I viewed the scintillating colors of His rainbow, I could begin to see that this rainbow was indeed present even during my darkest nights.

My graduation was right around the corner, and all the last minute details for the big event were well underway. We ordered a huge cake to serve fifty, and my dear friends signed up to bring food and to help with set up and tear down after the party. Some friends had also graciously offered to host my out-of-town family members in their homes, since Dave and I only had room in our home for my mother, Cathy, and her son.

I invited all the relatives to come to our house to eat together the night before graduation, and I made sure that we had plenty of food. Yet my mother kept insisting that I buy extra food, which didn't make any sense since we knew exactly how many people would be present. She laughed and said that Esther's son Mike was a growing boy and would probably have a big appetite. At my mother's insistence, at the last minute I ordered extra stromboli. Just a couple minutes after they were delivered, I saw someone walking down the sidewalk. At first I didn't know who it was, but soon I realized it was Esther's oldest son Joey from Chicago! That was a wonderful surprise. But then a couple of minutes later I saw someone else walking towards our house. As I strained to see who it was, I realized that it was my sister Esther! I thought I was in the middle of a dream and that I must be imagining things. But when she walked into our yard, I burst into shouts and tears of joy as I understood that she had decided to surprise me! Now I knew why Mom kept insisting that I order some extra stromboli. My heart was very full, and I was now ready to enjoy one of the biggest days of my life.

I certainly felt the Lord's tender love as He took great delight in me, and could almost hear Him "rejoicing over me with singing!"

Exploring Chapter 11

My Thoughts

When we finally decided that we were not going to have children, I had a choice. Would I allow childlessness to define me, to create bitterness, and to cause me to resent my husband? Certainly not. With the Lord's help, I chose to accept His will for my life, and determined to pursue my passion to counsel hurting people as a social worker.

Your Turn

Has the Lord asked you to accept His will for your life, even though it was not your heart's plan? Did you choose to be bitter, or allow Him to make you better? How did you surrender to His plan?

Chapter 12
Forgiveness is a Process, Not an Event

"And when you stand praying, if you hold anything against anyone, forgive them, so that your Father in heaven may forgive you your sins."　　　　Mark 11:25

*I*t was exciting to have so many friends and family arrive for this special occasion. May 16, 1993 was a joyous event, from the bagpipe processional on the beautiful grounds of Bryn Mawr to my own cheering section as I crossed the stage to receive my diploma. My gracious friends prepared the food and set up the sanctuary for the reception, and both family and friends enjoyed catching up with each other and "roasting" me during the reception.

This significant event was yet another indication that the Lord was helping me come to peace with my "new normal": *living life without having children.* Even though life was not what I expected, I could sense His hand of redemption as plans for my future were unfolding. I could feel my desert come to life as it was watered by His streams, and I was beginning to truly understand that He did indeed have a very specific plan for my life.

"The desert and the parched land will be glad;
the wilderness will rejoice and blossom ...
Water will gush forth in the wilderness
and streams in the desert.
The burning sand will become a pool,

the thirsty ground bubbling springs ...
And a highway will be there;
it will be called the Way of Holiness;
it will be for those who walk on that Way ...
But only the redeemed will walk there,
and those the Lord *has rescued will return.*
They will enter Zion with singing;
everlasting joy will crown their heads.
Gladness and joy will overtake them,
and sorrow and sighing will flee away."

Isaiah 35:1,6,7, 8-10

It was hard to say good-bye to everyone after the festivities ended, but I rested in His love with a heart full of gratitude that so many loved ones had come from far and wide to celebrate this significant milestone in my life.

I took the social work licensure exam while still in graduate school and passed it. At age 43, diploma in hand, I was licensed to practice social work in the state of Pennsylvania. Renewal Counseling, where I had completed my internship, hired me to work full time after graduation. I worked with couples, families, and individuals. It was such a blessing to have the opportunity to work in a faith-based agency where I would be free to integrate Scripture and prayer with the therapy process. I loved the experience of coming alongside the clients that the Lord had handpicked for me. It was a privilege and an honor, and over the next few years, I became more confident in my role as a therapist.

But my relationship with my mother remained rocky. I had never connected well with her. Even after her leukemia diagnosis, and even after my graduation, we still continued to struggle in our relationship. Throughout most of my adolescence, my mother had found the demands on her life to be extremely stressful in her role as the wife of the Superintendent of the Mental Health Institute. She had been unavailable for me on an emotional level. As a result, I had never felt close to her, and since Dad died, we both had increasing difficulty relating to each other. My visits to see her in Arizona were very tense, and I would come home feeling confused, angry, and sad. I knew in my heart that I was having trouble forgiving my mother, but I felt helpless to change the dynamic.

One Friday evening at *Beth Yeshua*, David Chernoff preached a sermon about the need to forgive those who have hurt us. After the service there was an opportunity to come forward for prayer. I felt a tug from the Holy Spirit to request prayer, but I wasn't certain that I was ready to forgive my mother. I obeyed the Holy Spirit's prompting, and ended up in line for prayer with one of our elders, Jeff. When this man of wisdom asked me how he should pray, I told him that I knew that the Lord wanted me to forgive my mother, but that my heart was not yet willing. He wisely exhorted me, "I suggest that you spend some time alone with the Lord and ask Him to show you how to forgive your mother." Immediately the Lord quickened that word to my heart, and I knew that it was something that I could receive and accept. Jeff prayed for my willingness, and I went home with hope that forgiveness was a possibility.

The next morning during my devotional time, I sensed that the Lord had a word for me. As I sat quietly in His presence, He lovingly challenged my heart: *"Would you be willing every day to begin loving your mother a little more, and resenting her a little less?"*

I was baffled initially, because I didn't think I actually resented my mother. Yet I knew right away this had come directly from the Lord to my heart. The Lord helped me to understand that since I had been unwilling to forgive my mother, I had opened the door for a root of bitterness to take hold in my heart. In obedience, every morning for the next several months I prayed that simple prayer, trusting that the Lord would help me one day to totally forgive my mother. As I prayed, I began noticing small changes over time. I was beginning to feel a little more love for my mother, and a lot lighter in my heart every day.

One Sunday morning in September of 1995, I woke up and realized that I was filled with love for my mother. All the hurt, bitterness, self pity, and anger no longer had a hold on me. Over time, I had experienced the power of forgiveness as a process, not a one-time event. Since real change takes place in the pathway of the heart, I knew unequivocally that it was genuine.

I recognized that I needed to take action as an act of faith. My mother had been battling leukemia, but at the time it didn't appear that it would take her life in the near future. However, the doctor warned us that she would eventually die from this disease. She was having regular blood transfusions and infusions, but she was becoming increasingly weaker as her white and red blood cells were battling against each other. I determined to call her and share my heart with her.

When I called and heard her voice, I was filled with so much love that it was hard to contain. I asked my mother to please forgive me for any hurt I caused her. I told her I had been harboring unforgiveness towards her for many years, and I wanted her to know that I had let it go and had nothing but a heart full of love for her. At that point I was crying and felt the cool breeze of the Holy Spirit washing over me. My mother spoke from her heart as well. She asked me to also please forgive her since she had been unable to be the mother that I needed her to be in my life. She admitted that all her energy had been consumed with my father and with having to keep up our image in the community.

We assured each other of our love, and when we hung up I felt so much peace. The Lord's timing is perfect, because little did I know that this would be the very last conversation we would ever have on this earth.

The following week, the doctor called me to tell me that the leukemia had worsened. I rushed to Arizona, as did my sisters Esther and Cathy, and my mother's sisters Henri and Sandy. September 26, 1995 my mother went home to the Lord. Esther and I had stayed in her room at the hospital and were actually with her the moment she took her last breath. We are both very deep sleepers, but the Lord woke us up in time to say good-bye and to tell her how much we loved her. It was a holy and very peaceful moment for both of us. We know it will be a joyous reunion when we see our mom in heaven one day.

"You who have shown me many troubles and distresses
Will revive me again,
And will bring me up again
from the depths of the earth."   Psalm 71:20

Exploring Chapter 12

My Thoughts

I resented my mother for not loving me the way I felt she should, and for not being the "Jewish" mother I hoped she would be. I am so very grateful that the Lord gave me the opportunity to forgive my mother before she died. His timing is always perfect, and it is such a blessing to know that we made peace and will see each other again in heaven one day.

Your Turn

Is there someone in your life that you have not yet forgiven? If so, what is the Lord saying to you about that relationship? What would it take for you to be willing to begin the process of forgiveness?

Chapter 13
Restorative Love

"Above all, love each other deeply, because love covers over a multitude of sins."   I Peter 4:8

After my mother's funeral, I headed back to Philadelphia. I gave myself some time to reflect and heal before jumping back into my work as a therapist.

Because of the resistance to the workshop on faith and social work, scheduling was delayed, but finally, in April of 1996, my supervisor and I presented the first workshop on *The Integration of Faith and Social Work* at the Bryn Mawr College Graduate School of Social Work. The participants were very receptive, and it opened the door for future workshops to continue. I am humbled and honored to have been granted this trail blazing privilege, paving the way for other interested social workers to offer faith-based counseling in their own practices.

An unexpected encounter with a young lady caused my life path to take another dramatic turn. We'll call her "Lucy" to respect her privacy.

I received a desperate call from Lucy asking for an appointment with me as soon as possible. As soon as she came into my office she burst into tears. Lucy shared that she was a Christian currently in college with a double major. She described herself as the "poster child" in her family and had been very involved in church in both the youth ministry and choir. When Lucy began her freshman year in college, she made a conscious decision to rebel against the high standards set by her family and church. She was tired of the pressure to continue in the role as the "perfect and obedient child". One thing led to another, and eventually she lost her virginity. When Lucy missed her period she was horrified to learn that she was pregnant. The thought of disappointing her parents and church family was beyond overwhelming. In her heart she knew abortion was wrong, but in a moment of desperation she made the decision to abort rather than risk the shame of facing her parents and church family.

Lucy went on to explain that as she was sitting in the waiting room at the abortion clinic, she began bleeding. Upon examination, the nurse informed her that she had just had a miscarriage. In that moment, Lucy knew that she had been given a second chance. She immediately repented and recognized the need for restoration and healing.

Lucy's mother had found a medical bill from the abortion clinic in Lucy's bedroom. Upon questioning, Lucy told her mom what had happened, and admitted that her intent had been to have an abortion. Her mother was devastated. After my initial meeting with Lucy, I suggested that we have a family session as part of the restoration process. Her family agreed.

During this family session, as Lucy wrestled with her crisis of faith, the presence of the Lord was palpable. She came to terms with the consequences of her decision to have sex outside of marriage and true repentance took place in her heart. Her parents also repented and apologized that they had expected so much from her and had put her up on a pedestal. Much healing occurred in that counseling room, as each member of the family took a turn expressing their feelings through their many tears. Each family member assured Lucy that they loved and forgave her, and their love covered over her sins. It was a beautiful picture of restoration, and Lucy committed her life back to the Lord.

After the family session ended, Lucy admitted to me that she felt the need for post abortion counseling. She knew in her heart that even though she had miscarried, because her intent had been to have an abortion, she needed to experience God's forgiveness and healing. I knew that Amnion Crisis Pregnancy Center in Bryn Mawr did post abortion counseling, and I was familiar with the Executive Director, Joan Boydell. I called and made an appointment for my client. I told Lucy that I would meet her there and introduce her to Joan. Lucy felt very comfortable with Joan and they agreed to meet for a few sessions.

As Lucy left Amnion, Joan called me into her office. What happened next was the sovereign hand of the Lord preparing me for a major change in direction that would shape His plan for my life calling.

Joan explained that the Board of Directors had approved the new position of Client Services Director, and that I had been recommended to her by a friend of mine who served on the Board. I was stunned and overwhelmed with this offer. I thought about my thriving private practice, and it didn't seem to make sense that I would leave all that behind and assume a full time position at a crisis pregnancy center.

Joan told me to think and pray about it, and if I was interested to call back and she would set up a time for me to meet with the Board. The Lord's ways are much higher than our ways (Isa 55:9). I would soon experience this Scripture in a very profound way.

When I went home that evening, I told Dave what had happened at Amnion. My husband by nature is very laid back, but what transpired next opened my heart in preparation to walk out my life calling. Dave asserted, "I believe if you don't follow through with this interview, you could regret this for the rest of your life." I recognized the sovereign hand of the Lord at that moment, so I didn't hesitate. I picked up the phone and told Joan I was interested in meeting with the Board of Directors.

"Faithful is He who calls you, and He will also bring it to pass."   I Thessalonians 5:24 NASB

We set up the appointment, and I arrived that evening not knowing what to expect. The Board president asked me to talk about how I could be helpful to the ministry at Amnion. What happened next was stunning. I prayed silently and asked the Lord to help me answer that question. Seconds later, tears started flowing and I began sobbing. In the twenty-seven years since my abortion, I had spoken very little about it. But right now in the boardroom I blurted out that I had had an abortion many years ago. I said that perhaps because of my painful experience, I would be able to come alongside other women who were contemplating abortion and guide them in their decision-making process. I also suggested that someday I could help post abortive women to heal from their abortion pain. I did not yet recognize my own need for healing.

The Board president thanked me for meeting with them and sharing my story. She prayed for me, and I left thinking I would never be offered the job. I had fallen apart emotionally, and could not imagine ever hearing from them again. After I got home and began telling Dave about the meeting, the phone rang. It was 10:30 at night, and I could not imagine who would be calling at that hour. Much to my surprise it was Joan Boydell!

Joan wanted me to know that the Board of Directors was very impressed with my credentials and life experience, and they unanimously agreed that I would be a perfect fit for the position of Client Services Director. Joan had the final authority as the Executive Director to offer me the job, and that is exactly what she did! I was shocked and overwhelmed and didn't know how to respond. She recommended that I take some time to pray and discuss it with Dave. She requested I call her back with my response in a couple days. Once again, my husband repeated his initial assertion, "If you don't accept this position, you may regret it for the rest of your life!"

But many questions remained. What would I do with all my clients? How could I end my private practice? How much time would I need to make this transition? Dave and I prayed and asked the Lord for wisdom and to make His perfect will for my life very clear now that this new offer was on the table. With grateful hearts, together in prayer, we committed it all into the Lord's capable hands, knowing that He would make it clear over the next couple days.

> *"Those who hope in the Lord*
> *will renew their strength."*   Isaiah 40:31

Exploring Chapter 13

My Thoughts
  It was such a privilege to come alongside Lucy during her crisis of faith as she came to terms with the consequences

of her decision to have sex outside of marriage. Little did I know that my meeting with Lucy would be the beginning of my life calling in the pregnancy resource ministry. I fought it at first, because it didn't make sense that I would leave my thriving private practice and pursue a full time job.

Your Turn

Was there a time in your life when you were suddenly faced with a decision that would require you to leave something important behind? What did you decide? Do you have any regrets?

Chapter 14
Delight in My Lord

"Delight yourself in the LORD;
And He will give you the desires of your heart."
Psalm 37:4 NASB

As Dave and I prayed about the job offer at Amnion, it became clear that the Lord was leading me to accept the position. We both felt peace about trusting that He would work out the circumstances ending my private practice. When I called Joan Boydell to tell her I would accept the position, she was delighted and willing to work with me to make a smooth transition away from my private practice. We agreed on waiting one month before I started working at Amnion full time so that I could have closure and transfer my clients to other therapists. Though I was sorry to end my time with my clients, I knew in my heart of hearts this was the Lord's will for the next season of my life.

I began working at Amnion in January of 1997. Joan informed me that because I had had an abortion in my past, I would be required to attend a post abortion Bible study before I could start meeting with clients. I didn't really think that was necessary at the time since the abortion had happened so many years ago, but because it was Amnion's policy, I agreed to attend.

There were seven other women who would be attending the study with me, meeting weekly for two hours over ten weeks. Joan and another professional counselor on staff would facilitate *Forgiven and Set Free* by Linda Cochrane. This Bible study uses Scripture and homework assignments to facilitate the healing process.

In the first few sessions, each of us shared our abortion stories. I was struck by the bonds that were formed as we opened up our abortion wounds to one another. In the beginning, most of us were guarded emotionally and perhaps still somewhat in denial. However, as we began delving deeper and getting in touch with the reality of our abortion decisions, the pain began emerging for each one of us.

One session during the course of the study, I came to the realization that I had made a decision to end my baby's life. The overwhelming feelings were so intense that I fell on the floor in gut wrenching sobs. I thought I would never stop sobbing. Even though my abortion had happened twenty-seven years before, it felt like it was yesterday. I was in shock, and whatever denial I had at the beginning of the Bible study melted away with every sob. Some of the other women had had more recent abortions and others had aborted many years ago, but they all had intense emotional reactions as well. We all felt so much shame and guilt and wondered how the Lord could ever forgive us for choosing to end the lives of our unborn babies. Thankfully our facilitators were skilled and full of compassion, love, and mercy.

One of the chapters in the Bible study covers forgiveness. Most post abortive women have difficulty forgiving themselves, and that was definitely true for each of us. Through the Scriptures it became clear that the Lord offers His forgiveness freely, but it is up to us to accept this gift.

We recalled how King David cried out to the Lord for forgiveness after his sins of adultery and murder:

"Cleanse me with hyssop, and I will be clean;
wash me, and I will be whiter than snow.
Let me hear joy and gladness;
let the bones you have crushed rejoice.
Hide your face from my sins
and blot out all my iniquity.
Create in me a pure heart, O God,
and renew a steadfast spirit within me."

Psalm 51:7-10

And we were reminded that God's command to forgive includes forgiving ourselves:

"So, as those who have been chosen of God, holy and beloved, put on a heart of compassion, kindness, humility, gentleness and patience; bearing with one another, and forgiving each other, whoever has a complaint against anyone; just as the Lord forgave you, so also should you."

Colossians 3:12-13

As we worked through the study, in time, we were able to receive His cleansing love and forgiveness. Before the final week of the Bible study, we held a memorial service to provide closure. Each of us decided how we wanted to memorialize our babies. Some brought poems, others wrote letters. I chose a song that spoke of God's redemptive healing.

It's interesting to note that though abortion is legal in our country, society has no way to address it. Women still suffer in silence, and there are no Hallmark cards expressing sorrow after an abortion. This memorial service helped to promote healing. It helped us to move the focus off our unborn children and on to the assignment the Lord has for us, to help others to receive the same comfort that we ourselves had received from the Lord.

"Praise be to the God and Father of our Lord Jesus Christ, the Father of compassion and the God of all comfort, who comforts us in all our troubles, so that we can comfort those in any trouble with the comfort we ourselves receive from God."   II Corinthians 1: 3-4

During the memorial service, we were instructed to ask God to reveal the gender of our babies. For me, it was the most challenging part of the service, because I had been in deep denial for decades.

As the Lord gently pulled back the curtain of my denial, the memory of my actual experience in the hospital came into vivid focus. Because my abortion had happened late in the second trimester, I had a saline injection, then went into labor and actually pushed the baby out. After the final push and splash into the bedpan, the nurse exclaimed, "Oh, you would have had a perfect baby boy!" Those words were so excruciating that it drove me to block them out for so many years. As the memory came crashing into my awareness, I could hardly accept her words, and they made the reality of my abortion even more devastating. It was only the Lord's overwhelming presence and mighty love that enabled me to revisit that memory. And over time, He brought His healing to my broken heart.

In the Jewish religion, it is customary to name your son after the first initial of your father's name. Since my father's name was Selig, I decided to name my baby Samuel, which means "God has heard". I do believe in my heart that the Lord has a special place in heaven for babies that have been aborted, and that one day the Lord Himself will introduce us. I believe this is also how King David was comforted when his baby died as a consequence of his sin of adultery with Bathsheba. David knew that one day he would return to his baby in heaven.

"I will go to him, but he will not return to me."
II Samuel 12:23b

After I got home, I told Dave about the memorial service, and that I had named my baby Samuel. I was overwhelmed by what happened next. Dave took me in his loving arms, and compassion poured out of his heart as he said, "I know Samuel is in heaven, but I would like to adopt him as my son." What a holy moment! Both of us felt the presence of the Lord in such a tender and loving way.

Since I would have no children on earth, this was truly another touch of the Lord's redemptive hand in my life. And now there is the glorious reality that Samuel, our son in heaven, will one day meet his parents.

Exploring Chapter 14

My Thoughts

I was not prepared to face my abortion, and I had no idea how deep the abortion wound affected my life until I began the post abortion Bible study. Even though processing through the myriad of emotions was a very painful journey, I am deeply grateful for the closure.

Part of my redemptive journey is the privilege over the years of coming alongside so many post abortive women in their healing process. What a blessing to see firsthand the Lord's restorative love, grace, and mercy in the lives of these dear hurting women.

Many of the women who have participated in the post abortive Bible studies desire to become facilitators to help other women who need healing after abortion. They have experienced the truth of the Lord's forgiveness, and desire to guide other women to freedom also.

Your Turn

Have you experienced an abortion in your life?
How has it affected you?

If you have not experienced abortion personally, do you know anyone who has? How can you offer grace and support?

> *Many pregnancy resource centers as well as local churches offer post abortion Bible studies to bring healing and freedom. Please see the Resources Section in the back of the book.*

Chapter 15
You Will Be a Mother to Many

"They looked to Him and were radiant,
And their faces will never be ashamed."
Psalm 34:5 NASB

*A*fter I completed the post abortion Bible study, I noticed right away that the shame and guilt had been lifted. I recognized that I was indeed forgiven, and now I was set free! *"So if the Son sets you free, you will be free indeed"* (Jn 8:36). I knew that I was ready to begin counseling other post abortive women, and that I could comfort them because I was now comforted.

As the Bible study ended, the Lord reminded me of the prophecy that I had received from David Chernoff the night we told him that we had decided not to have children: "Goldie, you will be a mother to many." His words didn't make sense at the time, but right now I was about to see that prophecy unfold.

At Amnion Crisis Pregnancy Center, I began counseling clients who came in seeking help in making decisions about their pregnancies. The Lord used my post abortion experience as a vehicle to help women understand that there may be emotional and spiritual consequences after abortion. If a woman chose abortion, Amnion welcomed her back for post abortion counseling. At this point in my career, I was more involved with pregnancy counseling than with post abortion counseling. Throughout my tenure at Amnion, I was privileged to come alongside many women who needed counseling and support throughout their pregnancies.

I had the joy of meeting many "Amnion" babies, and in some cases even participated as a support person in the actual birthing process. As the Lord allowed me to become "a mother to many", He showed me that this was all part of His unbelievable plan of redemption in my life. My need to nurture was definitely being met in my ministry to the young moms and their babies.

Although some women at Amnion decided to have abortions, many made decisions to either parent or make adoption plans. The adoption process provides the birth mother with a number of choices that offer some sense of ownership and control. Client Advocates provide clients with at least three adoption agencies, and clients choose the one that best suits their needs. The birth mother then chooses from various degrees of open adoption, or she could choose closed adoption. The birth mother is given several profiles of prospective adoptive couples, and eventually narrows it down to two couples.

She then meets face to face with both couples, choosing which couple will receive the gift of her baby. Both the birth mother and the adoptive couple receive counseling throughout the pregnancy, because the adoptive couples must be prepared for the possibility that the birth mother may change her mind after the baby is born. Depending on the state, the adoption doesn't become finalized until thirty to sixty days later.

The birth mother is instructed to write a letter to her baby explaining in simple and loving terms why she made the adoption plan. The intent of this letter is to minimize the feelings of rejection when the child eventually realizes he or she is adopted. Additionally, the adoption agency gives the adoptive family a teddy bear that has also been "adopted", with a little card telling the story from the bear's perspective. The adoptive parents give the letter and the teddy bear to the child when the child is old enough to understand the concept of adoption.

At the relinquishment ceremony, gifts are exchanged, prayers are said, and the birth mom is able to watch the adoptive couple holding and bonding with the baby. The birth mom leaves the hospital first, since it may be traumatic for her to watch the adoptive couple leaving the hospital with her baby.

One of the most poignant moments of my experience at Amnion involved a young lady with a bipolar diagnosis. I will call the client Marie for the sake of confidentiality. Marie was pro-life and did not want an abortion, and she desired to make an adoption plan. I was the counselor who would be helping her through the process. When I met Marie for the first time, she was very determined to go through with the adoption plan. This was uncharted territory for me, but I knew that the Lord would provide the necessary wisdom and grace as we embarked on this journey together.

I was shocked when Marie informed me that, due to her pregnancy, her doctor discontinued her bipolar medication. Having worked with untreated bipolar clients in the past, I knew that if she had a psychotic or manic episode it would be very dangerous. But miraculously, once Marie became pregnant, she experienced an extended period of lucidity. It appeared that the pregnancy hormones were protecting her from having any bipolar symptoms while she was pregnant! Marie saw it as a special gift of mercy from the Lord that allowed her to fully engage in the adoption process.

Marie continued to meet with me throughout her pregnancy, and also with her adoption counselor from the adoption agency. In our sessions together, Marie requested prayer, support, and help with anticipatory grieving. She knew that it would be heart wrenching to give birth and then say good-bye to her baby. Towards the end of her counseling with the adoption agency, I was invited to join them for a few sessions prior to the birth. The adoption counselor was very helpful in preparing us for what to expect on the day of the relinquishment ceremony.

Marie asked if I would be willing to be with her at the hospital on the day of relinquishment. Her parents and her adoption counselor would be there also. The birth father had signed away his rights and did not want to be present at the ceremony. I agreed to come, but with trepidation in my heart. Since I had aborted my own baby, I could not imagine the sacrifice Marie would be making, and didn't know how I would react. I made sure that we were all bathed in prayer, and I trusted the Lord to give me the grace to be supportive for Marie when the time came. She asked if I would arrive an hour before the adoptive family was due at the hospital so she could hold her baby and say her good-byes.

Marie knew that the adoptive family would choose their own name for her child, but she named her baby Faith. When I walked into the hospital room and saw Marie holding Faith, I was struck by how lovely they looked together. Faith was one of the most beautiful babies I had ever seen. She was just a couple days old but had a beautiful head of wispy blonde hair and sparkling blue eyes just like her birth mom. Marie was standing and holding baby Faith in her arms. She asked if I would come over and join the good-bye hug. As soon as I put my arms around Marie and the baby she burst into wrenching sobs. I held them silently in my arms, praying that I would not cry and that the Lord would pour His comfort and peace into Marie's heart. She wanted to release all her tears before meeting the family. Time seemed to stand still while I held them both in my arms for at least a half hour as Marie wept and poured out her heart.

Marie made a very powerful and unselfish decision to place her baby in the arms of a loving couple unable to have children of their own. I felt privileged and honored to be present during this holy exchange. By the time the family came into the room, Marie was peaceful and no longer crying. The adoptive couple expressed deep gratitude for the unselfish choice Marie had made on their behalf.

The adoptive couple recognized that due to Marie's bipolar illness, she would need to be back on her medication, and that seeing the baby from time to time would bring some measure of happiness for Marie. They had all agreed on an open adoption plan, which meant that Marie could spend time with the new family after a season of bonding took place.

I didn't expect the flood of emotions as soon as I got to my car. Watching Marie make such a loving sacrifice with her baby brought back feelings of remorse over my abortion. I wished I had had the courage to make an adoption plan. I admired Marie's choice. I admired my younger sister Cathy who also had an unplanned pregnancy and bravely decided to keep her baby. And my heart was also reminded of the ultimate sacrifice made by God the Father in sacrificing His only Son for our redemption.

"For God so loved the world, that He gave His only begotten Son, that whoever believes in Him shall not perish, but have eternal life."　　　John 3:16 NASB

I sobbed uncontrollably for quite some time, but I knew that the Lord was right beside me, wiping away every tear with His Fatherly love. I knew in my heart that

I was forgiven, and walking alongside Marie was another redemptive moment in my life.

About a month after the adoption was finalized, I received a beautiful letter from Marie. She thanked me for all the supportive counseling throughout her pregnancy, and for my presence at the hospital on the day of the relinquishment ceremony. She mentioned that shortly after the adoption she was admitted to a psychiatric hospital with a psychotic manic episode. She was back on her medicine and living at home with her parents. She ended the letter with this cogent statement: "In my mind I know I did the right thing, but my heart will forever tell me otherwise."

I'm sure Marie could identify with David as he penned these words:

"My God, my God, why have You forsaken me?
Far from my deliverance are the words of my groaning.
O my God, I cry out by day, but You do not answer;
And by night, but I have no rest."   Psalm 22:1-2 NASB

Marie and I continue to stay in touch, and to this day we send each other Christmas cards each year. I send her birthday cards as well. She doesn't see her daughter very often anymore, but has made peace with her decision. Marie is very grateful that her child is flourishing with her adoptive parents, receiving their love, nurture, and care.

"I will refresh the weary and satisfy the faint."
Jeremiah 31:25

Exploring Chapter 15

My Thoughts

The journey with Marie was a turning point in my counseling ministry at Amnion. Watching such a powerful and sacrificial exchange helped me to appreciate in a whole new way how adoption is such an unselfish and loving option for women experiencing unplanned pregnancies.

Your Turn

As you read about Marie's adoption experience, what feelings surfaced in your heart?

Were you ever led to sacrifice something or someone that was very important to you? How did you gain the courage to do it?

Chapter 16
The Gift of Family

"You are members of God's family."

Ephesians 2:19 NLT

I was blessed to serve in many positions over the years at Amnion Crisis Pregnancy Center, including Client Services Director, Director of Operations, and Executive Director. It was quite fulfilling and I learned much about the myriad of issues surrounding unplanned pregnancies.

At age 52 I found myself back in school. Amnion blessed me by funding a two-year certification program in biblical counseling at Christian Counseling Education Foundation. Through this program, I learned that real change takes place in the pathway of the heart. I discovered the importance of helping clients to go deeper than merely the level of emotional insight in the counseling process. As I put this training into practice, I found that encouraging them to seek heart transformation provided more lasting change in the clients' lives.

Upon graduation, I was asked to write an article about ministry in the crisis pregnancy center for *The Journal of Biblical Counseling*. The article, entitled "Jesus Rewrites Our Stories: Counseling in a Crisis Pregnancy Center", was published in the 2003 Spring Edition. I also had the privilege of speaking on this topic at the National Conference sponsored by the Christian Counseling Education Foundation.

In the 28 years we lived in Philadelphia, the Lord placed us in spiritual families, and we were always invited to spend holidays with dear friends. But deep in our hearts, we missed not having our family nearby, and whenever time permitted, we would drive up to Connecticut and spend time with Dave's family.

My family also lived quite a distance away, and we would see them only very occasionally. I felt especially close to Aunt Henri and my cousin Ellen because of the season they took me into their home when I was in my early twenties. At this point, Ellen and her daughter Kelly had moved to Florida. Aunt Henri and Uncle Paul had also moved to Florida years ago for their retirement; Uncle Paul died the same year my mother went home to the Lord. I didn't have much contact with my relatives over the years, but I always held them close to my heart.

I took a trip down to Florida with my friend Shelley and reconnected with Aunt Henri and Ellen. They mentioned that they were planning on taking a cruise with the family and suggested that Shelley and I join them. I had never cruised before, but my parents loved cruises and had taken many together over the years. I laughed at first since I thought cruises were for older people! But Ellen assured me that people of all ages loved cruising and encouraged me to give it a chance. Little did I know what amazing doors would open down the road, but with a sense of adventure I accepted my cousin's invitation. Dave was not the least bit interested in cruising, but encouraged me to go. My friend Shelley also decided to give it a try, and we had a blast. From the moment I got on the ship until the moment we docked, I was mesmerized. I could not stop videotaping, and I simply fell in love with the cruise experience. But even more significant was the blessing of reconnecting with Ellen and the rest of the family.

Ellen and I continued to stay in touch after the family cruise, and when I received a call from her a few years later, an exciting new chapter opened up in my life. Ellen's work as a travel agent involved planning theme cruises. She asked me if I would come aboard as Entertainment Director on an *Elvis Tribute Cruise*. She knew that I had a musical background, and thought I would enjoy this new role. All my expenses would be paid, so it was a no-brainer. My childhood dream of becoming a Cruise Director like Julie on the television show *The Love Boat* was coming true! I had to improvise my new role as Entertainment Director, but since I was accustomed to performing and loved people, I fell into the role naturally. The door was opened for many more cruises with Mahwey Productions, LLC and *Cruising with the King*. I would need to write another book to share about all of our lively and exciting adventures!

It became clearer every day that I had found my life calling in the pregnancy center ministry. My need to nurture was being fulfilled, and the Lord continued His redemptive work in my life. The pain associated with our decision not to have children faded as each day passed. I had a sense of purpose, and no longer felt the deep longing to have a baby. The Lord had other plans for our lives, and I was ready to move on.

Through my ministry at Amnion, I began corresponding with the director of a crisis pregnancy ministry in Israel called *Be'ad Chaim*, or "Pro-Life". She asked if we would be willing to bring a team from Amnion to help train her counseling staff. In 2007, some of Amnion's generous donors made it possible to send a six-person team to Israel: Amnion's Executive Director Joan Boydell and her husband Bruce, myself as the Client Services Director, a male counselor, and two presenters from our Relationship Education Team. Since my sister Esther knew the director of *Be'ad Chaim*, she arranged our accommodations and agreed to be our tour guide, helping us to understand the Israeli culture. *Be'ad Chaim* provided translators, and we ministered all over the country. The *Be'ad Chaim* counselors and the Israeli youth were very responsive to our teaching. The director of *Be'ad Chaim* was blessed by the fruit from our training, and we all felt the hand of the Lord in a powerful way.

During the trip, I had the opportunity to share my post abortion story to a group of counselors who ministered to women all over Israel. According to Joan Boydell's husband Bruce, I shared with so much passion that it became obvious to him that post abortion ministry is my true calling. He went on to say that one day this would most likely be the focus of my ministry. I couldn't see it at the time, but I held his words in my heart. It seemed to be prophetic, and I sensed in my spirit that I needed to take it seriously.

> *"A word fitly spoken is like apples of gold*
> *in settings of silver."*   Proverbs 25: 11 NKJV

Exploring Chapter 16

My Thoughts

I was surprised to hear the word that one day I would be more involved in the post abortion ministry. At that point in time I wasn't interested in ministering directly with post abortive women. But I knew to keep this exhortation close to my heart and trust that the Lord would reveal His perfect will in due time.

Your Turn

Was there ever a time in your life when you resisted a potential ministry or work opportunity? If so, what was holding you back? Did you eventually surrender to His call?

Chapter 17
The Stage is Set

"I will refresh the weary and satisfy the faint."
Jeremiah 31:25

*A*fter sixteen months as Executive Director of Amnion, the demands had become overwhelming. It became clear to me that I was weary and fast approaching burnout. I needed to step down and allow the Lord to refresh my weary soul.

In April 2007, when I made the decision to leave my position as the Executive Director, the Board of Directors offered me the position of Center Director for one of our locations. Besides management responsibilities, I was responsible for the supervision and training of counselors, including staff, interns, and volunteers. I loved this new role and it was a welcome respite from the burdens I carried as Executive Director.

One of the highlights of this new position was the birth of a ministry for parents of teenagers who had become pregnant. I founded this support group, and co-facilitated it with a male therapist on staff. The focus of the group was to offer support for the *parents* of pregnant teenagers and of teenagers who had become parents themselves. We called it POPPY, Parents Of Pregnant/Parenting Youth. It was such a joy to come alongside these dear parents in their journey with their kids. They learned new healthy coping skills while coming to terms with their "new normal". Their goal was not to enable, but rather to support and empower their kids to assume their own responsibility as new parents. The participants benefited greatly from the mutual support and deeply bonded with one another. Quite a few parents attended regularly, and the program continued for several years, until the end of my tenure at Amnion.

When the financial recession hit in 2008, many people were unable to continue donating to charities at the same level, and nonprofit organizations and ministries suffered greatly. Amnion Crisis Pregnancy Center was no exception, and the loss of income necessitated layoffs. Suddenly, at age 59, I found that my position would be cut from full to part time. Besides losing the income, I would also lose my health insurance.

I heard from a colleague that Hope Pregnancy Center in Philadelphia was looking for someone to assume the role of Client Services Manager. I was offered the position, and began working part time at Hope while also remaining at Amnion part time.

Hope Pregnancy Center was located in the heart of the inner city of Philadelphia, and was quite a culture shock for me. But as I came to know the founder, Herbert Lusk, and understand his heart and his vision, it didn't take me long to fall in love with the staff and clients of Hope.

Herbert Lusk, the "praying tailback" who would kneel in the end zone to pray after a touchdown, left his lucrative position with the Philadelphia Eagles in 1978 to serve those less fortunate in the heart of inner city Philadelphia. A visionary with a passion and heart for the poor in his community, Reverend Dr. Herbert Lusk became Senior

Pastor of Greater Exodus Baptist Church, and in 1989 founded *People for People*, a ministry to break the cycle of poverty in the inner city. *People for People* battles crime, drugs, and hopelessness, serving all ages, from children to adults. In order to provide support and hope for those in need, this ministry provides a whole array of social service programs, such as education, job training, counseling, mentoring, nutritional services, and affordable housing.

Pastor Lusk's motto is "from the cradle to the grave". In 2008 he had a vision to birth the Hope Pregnancy Center as a beacon of hope to provide support and help to women and their families facing unplanned pregnancy. Many women in unplanned pregnancies felt that abortion was their only choice. But with Hope Pregnancy Center sandwiched between so many support services, adding free ultrasounds and counseling to the many other community resources, it was now a viable option for these women to consider carrying their babies to term.

In December of 2009, Dave and I decided to take a little vacation to Florida to enjoy the warm sunshine and spend some time with my family. We stayed at a motel in downtown Delray Beach. One morning over breakfast at a quaint café, I found myself saying to Dave that if we ever had to move anywhere, I could see us living in Delray Beach. I loved all the cute boutique shops and outdoor cafes along Atlantic Avenue, but the crème de la crème was the beautiful beach! Truly the beach has always been my "happy place". I tucked this desire in my heart, hoping that perhaps one day it just might happen. Little did I know that by stirring this desire within me, the Lord was setting the stage to unfold His will for my life.

In August of 2010, I was hired fulltime as the Client Services Manager at Hope Pregnancy Center. Leaving my part time job at Amnion was bittersweet. My time at Amnion was full of profound memories of transformation and healing, and I so loved the staff and volunteers. But clearly I saw the Lord's hand and His goodness in providing fulltime work at Hope, which also included health insurance benefits.

> *"I will sing to the Lord,*
> *Because He has dealt bountifully with me."*
>
> Psalm 13:6 NASB

I already had a wonderful rapport with the staff and volunteers, and enjoyed their loving support. But the greatest blessing was falling in love with the African American community. It was such a joy to drive into work each day, for Hope Pregnancy Center was a brilliant light in this community and such an exciting place to work.

When I first began working there, Hope was just making the transition from a pregnancy counseling center to a medical clinic, and had recently procured an ultrasound machine and hired a Nurse Manager. Many women chose life for their babies as they received counseling and medical services, as well as support from *People for People* and Exodus Baptist Church.

My role as Client Services Manager involved counseling women in crisis pregnancies, as well as training and supervising new volunteers. I also helped and encouraged some post abortion clients through the abortion recovery Bible study. Most memorably, I bonded very deeply with the staff and volunteers as they took me under their wings and helped me to adapt to the culture. Pastor Lusk commented that he noticed how well I had become a part of the African American culture and considered me to be an integral part of the Hope "family".

Although things were going well for me, this was not the case for Dave. His body had suffered quite a bit of wear and tear during all the years of hard labor in the janitorial business, so he had transitioned into computers. Although initially his computer business was profitable, with the loss of his business partner due to health conditions coupled with the economic downturn in 2008, the business was markedly affected. Since we were dependent upon both incomes in order to meet monthly expenses, things had begun to get quite difficult financially.

In December of 2010, we took another short trip to vacation in Florida and spent time with my side of the family. My cousin Ellen recommended that we meet with her accountant to discuss our financial situation and perhaps get some objective advice. The accountant was shocked to see the host of self-employment taxes we paid in Pennsylvania. He strongly encouraged us to consider moving to Florida, pointing out that both taxes and cost of living expenses are considerably lower than in Pennsylvania.

Ellen strongly encouraged us to move to Florida too. She thought that we would be a lot better off financially, and we would also be close to family. I was open to the idea, but at that point, Dave was not. Our trip to Florida turned out to be a tense visit because of our divergent thoughts concerning a move. But over the years, we had learned to pray when we don't agree. We sought the Lord for guidance and clear direction. I told Dave how much it would mean to me if we lived closer to family, especially since we don't have children. Additionally, Dave's brother and wife also lived in south Florida. Even though it had been many years since we had heard from them, I hoped that Dave might have the opportunity to reconnect with his brother if we made the move.

When we headed back to Pennsylvania, we had not made a decision yet, but we agreed we would continue to pray and seek the Lord. We asked our friends at our congregation to join us in prayer. I also met with Pastor Lusk and asked him to pray for us. After he prayed, he had a word for us. He felt that the Lord was going to be moving us to Florida for rest, family, and worship. He added that the Lord would make it very clear to us when the time was right. Our lease on our apartment was up for renewal by August 1, 2011. The rent was escalating again, and it was more than we could afford.

Dave and I decided that I would return to Florida and explore the rental market. I had my heart set on Delray Beach, and our realtor lined up several properties for me to see. One in particular stood out above all the others: a renovated condo in an over-fifty-five community.

The property around the condo was beautiful. It was lined with gorgeous trees, and boasted a walking path and a lovely lake behind the condos. The two-bedroom two-bath condo was very bright with an open concept and a screened in porch. I was surprised to find such a lovely condo for half of what we were paying in Pennsylvania!

I took pictures and e-mailed them to Dave. He was pleasantly surprised when he saw how lovely it was, and was shocked to learn that we would be paying half the rent we had been paying in Pennsylvania. He agreed that we should act quickly, so I notified the realtor that we were definitely interested. She assured us that she would contact the landlords immediately and let them know. We felt the urgency to make a decision in order to give notice to our landlord in Pennsylvania.

There would be many details to be worked out, but we knew the Lord would make it very clear, just as Pastor Lusk had said in his word to us. Just maybe the Lord had heard the desire of my heart in that quaint café two years ago, when I dared to dream that perhaps one day we would be living in beautiful Delray Beach.

"Delight yourself in the LORD;
And He will give you the desires of your heart."
Psalm 37:4 NASB

Exploring Chapter 17

My Thoughts

Over the years, Dave and I had learned to go to the Lord together in prayer before making any decisions. We also sought wise counselors to pray with us. Praying and waiting on His answer would take us from confusion to clarity.

Your Turn

How do you handle making important decisions? Do you have wise people in your life that you can go to for advice?

Chapter 18
A Leap of Faith

"Now faith is confidence in what we hope for, and assurance about what we do not see."　　Hebrews 11:1

As Dave and I continued to pray, it was becoming clearer each day that the Lord was leading us to make the move to Florida. I marveled at how He was putting all the pieces of the puzzle in place and truly making a way for His purposes to be accomplished. He only required us to have open and obedient hearts.

We had to consider what type of work to pursue once we moved to Florida, not only to keep active, but also to bring in extra income. At 60, Dave did not intend to start up another business venture. I was 62, and we could both start collecting early retirement from Social Security. This would provide a steady source of monthly income, but it would not be enough to pay all the bills.

On my many visits to Florida over the years, my cousin Ellen and I often visited Light House Cove, a gorgeous beach resort in Pompano Beach. On one Sunday afternoon, there was a duo performing at the resort in the Tiki Bar. They sang together and played sax and flute – the same instruments Dave and I play. Listening to them inspired me to consider the possibility of the two of us forming a similar performing duo when we were settled in Florida.

At the time, I had no idea how it could possibly happen, or if Dave would even be open to the idea. But because so many creative ideas and answered prayers have taken place at Light House Cove, I felt that it was an epiphany from the Lord.

When I returned to Pennsylvania, I broached the subject with Dave. He is very practical, and could not possibly imagine how we would make this happen. I suggested that we just purchase some background tracks and start working out some musical arrangements. I told him that we had nothing to lose, and it could be a source of income after we made our move to Florida. Somehow, he was convinced.

Once we had several songs under our belt, we invited some of our friends over for a trial performance. The show set list included my sax and Dave's flute. Our friends loved it and believed we had great potential as a musical duo. Fern, a very dear friend and member of our worship team, came up with the name for our duo. She exclaimed, "It's a no-brainer. You should call your duo *The Winn Winn Situation!*" She was so excited about the name that she offered to design our logo, business cards, and address labels as our send off gift!

Another friend suggested that we consider performing a show for the residents in our apartment building in Pennsylvania. She reasoned that since most of the residents in our apartment building were seniors, and because there are so many retirement communities in Florida, that performing for our Pennsylvania apartment building residents would be a good test.

Our first performance was met with such an enthusiastic response that we were motivated to learn new songs and focused on improving our show. We continued to host performances, seeking objective feedback from the audience. Yet taking our show to Florida, where we would be completely unknown, would truly be a leap of faith.

We were approaching the deadline to give the required three-month notice to renew or terminate our current lease. We scheduled a phone interview with the Delray Beach condo owners, who promised that they would let us know by the end of the week if they had chosen us to rent the condo. It was exciting, but at the same time unsettling, because we didn't know what the future would hold. The deadline was fast approaching, and we were anxious to receive an answer soon.

A few days later, our realtor called to notify us that the landlords were very impressed. They loved our high credit score, they had enjoyed talking to us, and they definitely wanted to be our new landlords! We were pleasantly surprised and told her we would gladly rent the condo effective August 1, 2011. That gave us three months to work out all the details of the move. Miraculously, our new landlords graciously agreed to wait on the security deposit until we had received the security deposit back from our current lease.

We had no idea what would await us as we prepared to transition into our special new home in Florida. Would it truly be our earthly paradise? My dream to one day live in Delray Beach was fast becoming a reality, and I was filled with gratitude that the Lord had heard and answered my heart's desire.

"My presence will go with you, and I will give you rest."   Exodus 33:14

Exploring Chapter 18

My Thoughts

The Lord was stretching our faith as He called us, both without jobs, to move to Florida. He stretched our faith even further as He led us to form a performing duo and trust Him for income.

Your Turn

Has the Lord ever given you a creative idea and called you to take a risk? Did you leap into the water, or step in gingerly, one toe at a time? What bolstered your faith as you proceeded forward in His plan?

Chapter 19
Earthly Paradise

"Trust in the LORD and do good;
dwell in the land and enjoy safe pasture."

Psalm 37:3

e gave the management company notice that we would be vacating the apartment, and began the arduous process of packing. We had lived in the Philadelphia area for twenty-eight years – longer than any other place where we had ever lived. We had no relatives living in the area, and many loving friends had become like family. I was very fond of my job at Hope Pregnancy Center, and dreaded having to say good-bye to the many dear ones that I had come to know and love very deeply over the years that I was employed there. We couldn't even imagine the heartache of having to say good-bye to so many cherished friends, but we knew that the Lord was calling us to make this move. We trusted Him to provide the grace necessary when it came time to leave.

In order to make the move easier, some of our belongings and furniture we gave away, and some we sold. We still needed additional money for the move, so we decided to sell one of our cars and figure out how to get by with just one car. Over the years, we have learned that when the Lord is leading us to make a change, He will work out every detail, for *"faithful is He who calls you, and He also will bring it to pass"* (I Thess 5:24 NASB).

Ellen's brother John, who lived in Maryland, heard that we were selling our Ford Focus, and thought it would be a perfect car for his son Joey. As God would have it, *Cruising with the King* was scheduled to leave out of Baltimore in July. I drove to Baltimore for the cruise, and John decided he would drive back to Pennsylvania with me after the cruise to purchase the car! What an amazing answer to prayer and provision as the time of our move was pressing closer. Everything was falling into place.

In the weeks before we left, we spent time with as many people as we possibly could. Our congregation had a special and touching send-off service, complete with an *Oneg Shabbat*, or Joy of the Sabbath, in our honor. Joyful yet bittersweet, it was full of many prayers, songs, gifts, delicious food, and plenty of tears. This congregation had truly become a special spiritual family to us for so many years, so it was very sad to leave them. The warm weather in Florida was our only consolation, for we knew that some of our friends would come down to visit in order to escape the winter cold.

Dave and I also held a final show at our apartment building, inviting all our friends. They enjoyed our show and encouraged us to continue performing in Florida. With food and good-bye cards they gave us a loving and memorable farewell, but our hearts were heavy as we said good-bye to these endearing friends.

We procured a moving company and loaded the van; it would be about two weeks before everything arrived in Florida. We decided that Dave would head down to Florida first. I would stay and work one more week at Hope Pregnancy Center, and then head to Florida on the Amtrack, bringing our car and some of our more essential belongings. Our family was so very excited that we would be joining them in Florida, and assured us that they would do everything they could to help us make a smooth transition.

The time to embark on the next stage of our journey drew near. I drove Dave to the airport, and it suddenly dawned on me that he had a one-way ticket to Florida in his hand. Before this moment, it had all seemed ethereal, like I would soon wake up and realize that I had been dreaming. But once I said good-bye to my beloved husband and started driving away from the airport, I suddenly realized that it was very real.

We were about to receive a huge surprise upon our arrival to Florida. Through a series of God-ordained connections, we discovered that our dear friends from *Beth Yeshua*, Rick and Sherry Heller, were now living in Delray Beach! We had always said that if we ever lived near each other, we would surely be close friends. But I never dreamed that we would connect again – let alone live in the same city! Rick and Sherry were so delighted that we were moving to Delray Beach, and offered to help in any way possible. When they welcomed Dave to Florida before I arrived, we found that we would be living only five minutes from each other!

I prepared for my last days at Hope Pregnancy Center, and packed up the car for the auto train. During my final week, I stayed with my precious friend Rhona, who had so many years ago walked with me through that dark season of releasing my desire for children to God. This was truly the end of a dynamic era, and an intriguing new adventure was about to begin. Dave and I had taken a huge step of faith, but we knew with certainty that we had trusted an *unknown* future to a *known* God.

"The Lord directs the steps of the godly.
He delights in every detail of their lives."
Psalm 37:23 NLT

Exploring Chapter 19

My Thoughts

It was so painful to say good-bye to so many treasured friends. But the Lord kept giving us confirmations, from the smooth sale of the car to the very affordable condo to Rick and Sherry living only five minutes away. His obvious hand on each detail gave us the much needed reassurance that He was indeed directing our steps.

Your Turn

Was there a pivotal time in your life when the Lord called you to step out in faith? What do you remember most about that experience?

Chapter 20
Test of Faith

*"I will go before you
and make the rough places smooth."*

Isaiah 45:2 NASB

*M*y family was so helpful when Dave arrived by himself in Florida. My cousin Ellen picked him up at the airport and helped him to get settled into the condo. She also made sure that he had enough household supplies to hold him over until the moving van arrived. My trip down to Florida on the Amtrak Auto Train was uneventful, and it was a blessing to finally reunite with Dave in our beautiful new home on August 9, 2011.

It was such fun getting reacquainted again with Rick and Sherry after so many years. They had arrived in Florida a year earlier and were attending *L'Chaim*, a Messianic Congregation in West Palm Beach. Rick and Sherry invited us to attend a service with them one *Shabbat*, and immediately we felt welcomed into the congregation.

L'Chaim was a small congregation without a live worship team. Rick had been leading worship, singing along with CD's. When the leaders found out that Dave and I were seasoned worship leaders, and that Dave played keyboard, they asked us if we would consider leading live worship. Rick was overjoyed to team up with Dave and me, and we began weekly rehearsals right away. Since we were grieving the loss of leaving our congregation after so many years, it was a blessing to be invited to lead worship, and certainly helped to fill the void.

Ellen had warned me that the transition to life in Florida would be difficult, but neither Dave or I could ever have guessed just how challenging it would be. Financially, things were tight. We had made the move by faith with only our Social Security checks and with no other income to fall back on. We would need to discover ways to bring in supplemental income, and that would take time. Yet during this time of transition, the Lord was ever so faithful. Friends back in Pennsylvania felt led to help us financially until we could get established. What a blessing it was to receive those checks in the mail when we least expected them!

Dave had a rough time adjusting in more ways than just the financial. He had always had a very strong work ethic, and when it suddenly hit him that he would no longer be working, it came as quite a shock. He wanted to feel productive, and wondered what he would be doing for the rest of his life. Dave has a gentle nature and such a tender heart, he is such a blessing to all those he encounters. He was making a difference, but somehow he felt that he needed productive work to in order to feel valuable.

My heart ached for Dave, and I so wanted to help him find purpose in this next season of life. I felt certain that if we could be successful with *The Winn Winn Situation*, it would help Dave feel that he did have purpose. I began to concentrate on marketing our duo, focusing on the niche market of assisted living and nursing homes. I interviewed a few activity directors and entertainers, and they suggested that we begin visiting some facilities and offer to perform free demo shows.

The Winn Winn Situation had their first breakthrough when an activity director at an assisted living home agreed to allow us to perform a free demo show. She promised that if the residents liked our show, she would set up future dates for us. We were both very nervous, but the residents were delighted with our show, and she booked us through to the end of the year! She also agreed to be our first reference in Florida for marketing to other facilities. This was a beginning, but I knew that this would require perseverance, and that it would take time to get our show on the road. I never gave up hope.

One of the ways I tried to encourage Dave during this difficult transition was by inviting him to walk with me in the lovely and peaceful nature areas near our condo every day. I knew that this would be a life-giving activity, and would also serve to help him acclimate to our beautiful new surroundings. My hope was that he would also begin to appreciate some of Florida's natural beauty while waiting for *The Winn Winn Situation* to get established. Dave also found it beneficial to meet with a therapist for extra emotional support during this transitional time.

I was hoping to find a part time job working in the crisis pregnancy ministry, which was still so dear to my heart. One *Shabbat* at *L'Chaim*, the leader held up a baby bottle and encouraged congregants to take one home and fill it up with coins to support First Care Women's Clinic in West Palm Beach. My heart leaped and I knew that was where I wanted to work.

My pastor's wife knew the Executive Director of First Care, and called on my behalf, asking her to consider hiring me. Surprisingly, I felt drawn to the post abortion ministry and was hopeful a position might be available. I was invited in for an interview with the Executive Director and the two program directors.

During the interview, they asked me what part of the ministry interested me. When I mentioned post abortion, they broke into smiles. That was exactly the position needed to complete the Programs Team at First Care! The ministry had recently experienced some strategic changes, and post abortion had become a priority. They assured me that they were definitely interested in hiring me, but confided that the budget was undergoing some changes, and there would be a delay. They promised to contact me at some point in the future.

I left the interview full of hope, and shared a little smile with the Lord as I remembered Bruce Boydell's prophetic word spoken to me years ago in Jerusalem, "One day you will be working in the post abortion ministry, since this truly is your passion." It was becoming increasingly clear that His plan of redemption for me included not only healing from my own abortion, but also an amazing opportunity to come alongside other hurting post abortive women who desire healing from their abortion wounds. He certainly had transformed my tears into joyful, purposeful work for His Kingdom.

> *"I will turn their mourning into gladness;*
> *I will give them comfort and joy instead of sorrow."*
> Jeremiah 31:13

Exploring Chapter 20

My Thoughts
The transition to our new life in Florida challenged us to walk in faith, focusing on the Lord and not on our

present circumstances. I knew in my heart that the Lord had a plan for our lives and that He was calling us to trust Him. He would unfold His plan in His perfect timing.

Your Turn

What is the faith-walk that the Lord has called you to right now? How do you keep your eyes on Him and avoid falling into the trap of worry?

Chapter 21
Abiding in His Presence

"I remain confident of this:
*I will see the goodness of the L*ORD
in the land of the living.
*Wait for the L*ORD*;*
be strong and take heart
*and wait for the L*ORD*."*   Psalm 27:13-14

These were challenging days as I waited to see if First Care would hire me. Months had passed by, and still no word. In the meantime I traveled to other assisted living facilities and was able to procure a couple more gigs for *The Winn Winn Situation.* Because we now had a Florida reference, it was no longer necessary to perform free demo shows, but we were told in no uncertain terms that if the residents did not like us, we would not be invited back.

I also interviewed several activity directors for ideas on songs that would appeal to the residents. They recommended that we perform a combination of songs from the 40's to the 70's. I also learned that keeping the music upbeat was key. We very slowly expanded our repertoire, and were gaining a little more confidence now that we had a few shows under our belt.

The lack of finances continued to be a burden. The

assisted living facilities would pay us four to six weeks after a show. Since I still hadn't heard from First Care, I was now fighting discouragement almost daily. It was so hard to be strong as I waited on Him.

One day during my devotional time with the Lord, I felt His presence in a palpable way. He challenged me to totally surrender our financial situation to Him, to trust that He would provide and would open whatever doors He had for us. In the quiet of the morning, as I gazed out of our Florida room to see the glorious sunrise, I cried out to the Lord. I asked for His forgiveness in not trusting that wherever He leads, He provides. Through tears I surrendered my hold on our finances and the job at First Care Women's Clinic. I sat in His presence for a few minutes, and He flooded me with His peace. It was a strengthening and restorative time of abiding in His sweet presence.

Minutes later, the phone rang. It was the Director of Programs at First Care. She apologized for taking so long to get back to me, and explained that there had been budget constraints and ongoing changes in the structure of the ministry. She went on to say that they were delighted to offer me the part time position that I had requested: Abortion Recovery Director!

I was ecstatic and immediately accepted the offer. I would begin working in a few weeks. Dave was delighted to hear the news, and we were beginning to see how the Lord was shaping our "new normal" day by day. Thanksgiving that year was particularly joyous, for not only was my heart overflowing with gratitude for my new job, but we also celebrated our first Thanksgiving with my family!

In December, my cousin Ellen's daughter Kelly was graduating from law school, and her wedding would be the day after her graduation! I am very close to Kelly, who affectionately calls me Mom #2. She is indeed a "daughter of my heart" and I am so very proud of her.

The beach wedding was stellar in every way, and family members and friends came from near and far to celebrate these extraordinary festivities. I was especially thrilled that my sister Esther had come all the way from Israel to attend Kelly and Mike's wedding. It was so much fun to show my sister around our new "hood". She is also a beach person and found Delray Beach charming.

Dave and I were beginning to feel more settled in our new life in earthly paradise. Florida is indeed the sunshine state, and it was so lovely to see blue skies, gorgeous foliage, beautiful beaches, and green grass all year round. Dave's depression was lifting slowly but surely with each passing day, and eventually he also began to reconnect with his brother.

I immersed myself into the job at First Care, and immediately felt like part of the family. I am blessed to work alongside so many Godly and loving people who are passionate about helping those who are facing unplanned pregnancies.

After I was trained for my position, the Director of Programs recommended that I participate in the Abortion Recovery Bible Study that First Care utilized, entitled *Surrendering the Secret*. I needed to become familiar with the curriculum they were using, since I would be training the facilitators and referring post abortive women to the study.

Although I have facilitated hundreds of post abortion Bible studies, I still receive more healing every time I participate in another one. I have often wondered about this, and have concluded that since women are designed to nurture life, having an abortion is a very deep wound to the soul. For many women, myself included, healing takes place layer by layer.

By the time 2012 rolled around, Dave was adjusting much better to life in Florida. He rehearsed for weekly worship services at *L'Chaim* and also for our performances at the assisted living facilities. We had been in Florida for five months, and *The Winn Winn Situation* was getting busier with new gigs. Performing for the residents was very rewarding because we could see how the music touched them. Because music memory is the last memory to be lost, when we perform in memory care facilities, the residents simply come to life as soon as the music starts. I felt that I had come full circle and now had the opportunity to put my music therapy skills to work in a whole new and fulfilling way. Dave and I had begun to flourish in our new home.

> *"But I am like an olive tree*
> *flourishing in the house of God;*
> *I trust in God's unfailing love*
> *forever and ever."* Psalm 52:8

Exploring Chapter 21

My Thoughts

The many months of waiting for First Care's job offer were fraught with anxiety for me.

Your Turn

What do you think the Lord was doing during that period of waiting? What do you think His purpose was in ordaining the delay?

Chapter 22
Embracing My Calling

"You will be like a well-watered garden,
like a spring whose waters never fail."

Isaiah 58:11

I flourished in my job at First Care, and it was hard to believe that for so many years I was not interested in serving in the abortion recovery ministry. It was almost as though I was running from my calling, and in some small way I could relate to Jonah. But I believe that during the years I evaded my calling, the Lord was doing a work in my heart to equip me for this restorative ministry.

I am very grateful to work with a dedicated team of post abortive women who are passionate about ministering to other women wounded by abortion. We have come to realize that abortion is truly a deep wound to the soul, and we still have a lot to learn about how to care for these women.

We have come alongside so many hurting women as they journeyed through the post abortion Bible studies. These women receive much healing, forgiveness, and freedom, and are able to truly close that chapter of their lives. It is such a joy to witness firsthand their transformation, as the shame and guilt disappear when they joyfully receive the Lord's deep and cleansing healing. Isaiah describes so poignantly the miraculous restoration:

"Giving them a garland instead of ashes,
The oil of gladness instead of mourning,
The mantle of praise instead of a spirit of fainting.
So they will be called oaks of righteousness,
The planting of the LORD, that He may be glorified."

Isaiah 61:3 NASB

The Lord has called many of these women to become abortion recovery facilitators themselves, to comfort others with the comfort they themselves have received (II Cor 1:4).

The next year was a time of grounding and peace with no major life events. We relished the time with our families, and fully appreciated the beauty of our new surroundings in Florida. As the buzz about *The Winn Winn Situation* spread by word of mouth, doors opened and we began performing in more senior facilities. Our repertoire continued to expand, and we seemed to have found the right balance of lively new songs and nostalgic old ones.

Music is a universal language, and its influence is very powerful. Even those who have lost much of their memory can still retain their music memory, and these dear seniors who have suffered losses on so many levels receive some lucidity and peace during our performances. The effect persists even after our performances, for our music seems to improve their overall well being. We began to realize the impact that our ministry was having when family members would thank us for bringing their loved ones some moments of happiness during our performances and even afterwards. Dave and I both began to comprehend what a blessing it is to bring musical joy to these sweet men and women.

I was grateful that after a very difficult transition for

Dave, it seemed that he had found purpose again. It was a blessing to see his musical talent blossom in his new role as an entertainer. Between *The Winn Winn Situation* and his work as worship leader, music had now become his main focus.

Looking back, I can see the Lord's hand of protection holding us fast during the few years it took to establish ourselves. Little did I know that I would soon be facing a very dark and challenging time in my life that would require me to trust and cling to the Lord as never before.

> *"If I rise on the wings of the dawn,*
> *if I settle on the far side of the sea,*
> *even there your hand will guide me,*
> *your right hand will hold me fast."*   Psalm 139:9-10

Exploring Chapter 22

My Thoughts

It seemed that I suddenly woke up to His call on my life, understanding that I was to minister to post abortive women. Although I laughingly call this a Jonah season, more accurately, it was a slow work of the Lord in my heart as He gently drew me into His plan. When I finally embraced His calling, I found it thrilling to partner with Him as He healed these broken women.

Your Turn

Have you had a Jonah experience? Are you in one now? Be still before the Lord and ask Him to reveal to you His gentle nudgings – or not so gentle ones – that are urging you into your calling.

Chapter 23
Freedom is a Choice

"When I remember You on my bed,
I meditate on You in the night watches,
For You have been my help,
And in the shadow of Your wings I sing for joy."
Psalm 63:6-7 NASB

Since my childhood, I walked through life in a fog. With the help of a psychiatrist, I later came to understand that I had experienced Post Traumatic Stress Disorder (PTSD) due to the unpredictability of my father's abusive behavior. It grew out of the fear that terror could interrupt me at any time, and it caused me to have difficulty getting started with daily tasks. Each morning it would take me a very long time to move out of the fog and settle down to the day's assignment. Much to my dismay, it appeared to others that I was simply procrastinating. This caused problems with my ability to focus in school, and later in life in my various jobs. Although the psychiatrist helped me to understand the problem, he offered no solution. To me, the fog was "normal". I assumed that it was just part of who I was, and I somehow learned to accommodate.

We moved to Florida to be closer to my family. But it never occurred to me that I would have difficulty trusting and learning how to behave in a family that is more functional than my own dysfunctional family of origin.

During our first two years in Florida, as we navigated the difficult transition, my family served as an anchor. It was delightful to celebrate all the holidays and birthdays together. I was especially close to my cousin Ellen, and we spent a lot of time getting to know each other in a deeper way. We also worked successfully as a team on *Cruising with the King* for many years.

As my sixty-fifth birthday approached, Ellen and her daughter Kelly wanted to plan a special 60's Party for this milestone birthday. I was so touched. However, my ideas for the party were very different than theirs, and as the planning began, conflicts arose. I was not aware of how I was reacting, but I learned later that I was reverting back to a helpless and vulnerable little girl. I was unable to trust their hearts for me, and started pulling away from the family. As I distanced myself, I caused much hurt and misunderstanding, and the party was in danger of being canceled entirely.

A few weeks before my birthday, Ellen invited me out to lunch. She shared with me that until recently, she couldn't fully comprehend my childhood experience. She admitted that since she lived far away from us, she knew very little about my father. When she came to visit, she had only seen his public persona. All she knew was that my father was very successful and that our family traveled extensively. She had never experienced the darker side of my father's personality. Over the years I had shared with her about our tumultuous family life, but she didn't begin to truly understand until we moved to Florida and she witnessed the detrimental effect it was having on my life so many years later. She explained that she now grasped that my childhood was very different than hers, and confided that her heart ached seeing how my father's physical and emotional abuse had affected me.

As Ellen acknowledged how she felt about my past, and disclosed her deep anguish for my pain, I truly knew in my heart how much she cared, and how she loved me unconditionally. I began weeping uncontrollably as pent up tears from long ago rose to the surface. I felt that I would never stop weeping. Ellen gently offered me compassion and reassurance. She reminded me how much she loved me and that she would help in any way she could.

When my tears subsided, she challenged me with this very profound question, "What would it be like for you to ask the Lord for total freedom from your past as His gift to you for your sixty-fifth birthday?"

All of a sudden I felt His sweet presence, as if my loving Heavenly Father was gently wiping away my tears. It was indeed a holy moment, and we sat in peaceful silence together for quite some time. But I wasn't quite sure I had the courage to take that step towards freedom.

A few days after my lunch with Ellen, when I was in my morning devotional time, the Lord led me to a Scripture which I had never seen before.

> "... *pour out your heart like water*
> *in the presence of the Lord.*" Lamentations 2:19

This Scripture captured how I felt when I wept that day at lunch with Ellen. As I pondered this Scripture, His loving presence wrapped around me in a deeply profound way.

Over the next few days, the Lord revealed to me that trust was the root issue that He desired to heal. He enabled me to understand that because I had never been able to trust my earthly father, it would be next to impossible to ever trust my family. Subconsciously, I did not want to risk further rejection, and keeping my distance would serve as self-protection.

The next day I had my weekly Skype call with my sister Esther in Jerusalem. I felt from the Lord to share with her what had happened at lunch the other day with Ellen. After we spoke, she prayed a beautiful sisterly prayer for me.

Esther counseled that the next step was complete surrender of the hold that my father had on my life all these years. She went on to say that the Lord would show me exactly where and when to surrender. She further cautioned that once I surrendered, I am to never look back. She explained that there is a Hebrew word *nikadot*, which means "period". My surrender is to be final and complete, just like a period at the end of a sentence. Esther assured me that I would clearly know that the healing has taken place, and that I would begin to experience daily freedom in my life.

Much to my surprise, the Lord moved very quickly after my prayer with Esther. That same afternoon, my dear friend Sherry and I headed to the beach. I had known Sherry for over thirty-five years, and we shared a deep bond of love, friendship, and trust. Sherry and I always walk in faith together on our excursions to the beach; we pray for good weather and a parking place and the Lord always provides. Today was no different. He gave us a perfect parking space and provided a beautiful sunny day. But no sooner had we pulled into the parking spot when out of nowhere a cloud appeared, and it began to pour. People were caught off guard and started quickly running for cover.

In the car with Sherry, I suddenly felt the palpable presence of the Lord and heard His still small voice say: *"Now! Now is the time to surrender, with your friend Sherry as your witness."* The Lord also let me know that after I surrendered, He would stop the rain, and that would be my sign, for the Jews require a sign (I Cor 1:22). Oh, He knew me so well.

I took a deep breath, opened my mouth, and prayed a heartfelt prayer of surrender, imploring the Lord to totally free me from any hurt, anger, and unforgiveness towards my father. I asked *Yeshua* to set me free from old family scripts and lies that I had believed about myself all these years. Every fiber in my being cried out to Him for deliverance from past bondage. With every fervent plea, I had total faith that He would set me free!

"So if the Son makes you free, you will be free indeed."
John 8:36 NASB

As soon as I finished the prayer, true to His word, the rain stopped immediately and the sun shone in all its brilliance. I knew that a miracle had just taken place. I was filled with a very deep peace – and I suddenly realized that everything looked clearer and brighter. I physically felt the Lord lift the burden of my past off me, and I knew without a shadow of doubt that I was completely set free!

When I awoke the next morning, something was dramatically different. The fog had lifted from my brain! My thoughts were clear and I did not have to wait for that fog to lift before pursuing my daily tasks. It took me a few minutes to grasp that the Lord had granted me a miraculous healing from the PTSD! I simply couldn't deny it. Suddenly things that used to be very difficult were easy. Johnny Nash's song *I Can See Clearly Now* took on a whole new meaning. It wasn't long before others in my life began to notice a difference in my countenance, my energy level, and my ability to focus. It was as though the deep joy of gratitude was radiating for all to see.

My sixth-fifth birthday was fast approaching, and I was now able let go of my expectations. Ellen and her daughter Kelly went to great lengths to make the 60's party very special, fun, and memorable.

When my friends came in from out of town for the party, they noticed a change in my countenance and commented that I had a special glow. I knew immediately my face was reflecting the Lord and His work within me.

> *"They looked to Him and were radiant,*
> *And their faces will never be ashamed."*
>
> Psalm 34:5 NASB

This gave me a unique opportunity to share with them my extraordinary healing journey, and I gave God all the glory! What a joy it was to thank my dear family and friends who had had a part in helping me to walk through this process.

As the weeks unfolded, I began to comprehend the magnitude of the gift the Lord had given me for my sixty-fifth birthday. I discovered that I was now no longer chained to lies about myself. Truth was readily apparent, and I had such clarity in both thoughts and actions. I was able to hear His voice more clearly, and I obeyed without delay. On that very special day in the parking lot with Sherry, the Lord had poured His showers of blessing upon my life and immersed me in His love - and my freedom came forth!

> *"Then you will know the truth, and the truth will set you free."*
>
> John 8:32

A very dear friend gave me a birthday present, a table plaque saying: "I love you to the moon and back." One morning shortly after my birthday party, during my quiet time, the Lord directed me to read the plaque out loud. He then let me know that this is how He, my loving Heavenly Father, feels about me: He loves me to the moon and back.

I burst into tears, but this time they were tears of gratitude and joy. My trust was restored, my heart accepted this truth, and I was able to fully receive this love from the Father's heart.

I had known intuitively that God would use my healing to bring comfort to others who are suffering, for this is indeed my life calling. Additionally, the Lord seemed to be revealing to me that He would be assigning me more challenging Kingdom work.

"From everyone who has been given much, much will be demanded; and from the one who has been entrusted with much, much more will be asked."   Luke 12:48

From the moment of my surrender and subsequent healing, the Lord deepened my desire to come alongside others who are suffering, reminding me that *"we love because He first loved us"* (I Jn 4: 19 NASB). He enabled me to understand in greater measure that my purpose is to be a hope-bearer, and my calling is to bring hope and encouragement to the broken. I am acutely aware that my capacity to love and care for others has markedly expanded since I fully surrendered my painful past to the Lord.

I had spent many years in this fog of hurt, anger, and unforgiveness towards my father. It seemed so much was lost during that time. But now, He was using the pain of my life and His marvelous restoration to reach others with His love, and was multiplying His Kingdom work in miraculous ways.

"So I will restore to you the years
That the swarming locust has eaten."
     Joel 2:25 NKJV

As I continued to walk out this great deliverance He

had given me, the Lord reminded me of a visit that I had with a friend the previous month. We had prayed together, and then the Lord had given her a vision that I was going to walk through an open door. Afterwards it would be forever closed behind me, never to be opened again. I realized that this prophetic word had been fulfilled when I had surrendered to the Lord. *Nikadot!*

My heart bursts with gratitude as a daughter of the King. He indeed is my help, and I sing with inexpressible joy under the shadow of His mighty wings. Glory to God!

Exploring Chapter 23

My Thoughts

This proved to be a pivotal time in my walk with the Lord. It required great courage and trust to renounce the lies and to totally surrender the anger and unforgiveness towards my father. I could not even imagine the unbelievable blessings that would meet me on the other side, but I did know that the Lord was calling me to be obedient.

Your Turn

What is the Lord calling you to place in His hands right now? Are you willing to obey Him?

Chapter 24
Nothing is Impossible With God

"But as for me, I watch in hope for the LORD,
I wait for God my Savior;
my God will hear me."   Micah 7:7

On the summer of 2015, when we were about to sign the lease to rent our condo for the fourth year, our landlords informed us of their intent to sell. They offered us the opportunity to purchase it before they put it on the market, but we were not financially prepared. Between the move from Philadelphia and the difficulty establishing ourselves in Florida, we had accumulated some debt. I sought the help of a mortgage lender who did everything she could to work with us, but buying a condo in Florida is not easy in the best of circumstances. To complicate matters, our debt to income ratio was too high, and even though we could afford the monthly payments, we didn't qualify for a mortgage.

At first we were greatly disappointed. We were so comfortable in our condo and didn't want to move. But we prayed and trusted the Lord for a perfect solution. We regretfully informed our landlords that we were unable to purchase their condo. They agreed to continue renting to us on a month-to-month basis. They needed time to put the condo on the market, and we needed time to find another place to live.

Hoping to find a less expensive condo to purchase, we

once again contacted our realtor. Together we looked at so many condos, but all of them were either too expensive or needed repairs beyond our budget. She asked us if we would consider renting again. There was a condo that was available in our same building just one flight above us. Since we had been so focused on purchasing, we hadn't even entertained the idea of renting again. After Dave and I prayed together, we felt a peace about moving forward, and asked her to set up a time for us to see the condo.

As soon as Dave and I walked in, we knew in our hearts that this was the Lord's provision for us, and we both felt a wondrous peace. The condo had been freshly painted, and new carpets had been installed throughout. I was elated to find that the Florida room was not simply screened in but was enclosed with glass, and I would be able to use it for my office all year round. There were a few minor repairs and cosmetic changes needed, and the landlords agreed to correct them. The final miracle was that the rent was less than we were currently paying! We asked our realtor to let the landlords know that we were interested, and we were soon signing a new lease.

When we met our new landlords, we felt an instant connection. Like Dave and I, Victor is Italian and his wife Norma is Jewish. They both love the Lord and know *Yeshua* as their Messiah. All four of us sensed the Lord's perfect timing in bringing us together. More miracles flowed forth as our new landlords assured us that they had no plans to sell the condo, and we could rent from them indefinitely.

> *"Behold, I am the LORD, the God of all flesh; is anything too difficult for Me?"* Jeremiah 32:27 NASB

We learned that Victor and Norma had strategically selected the location of this condo, choosing a higher floor in the middle of the building and a north/south exposure in case of hurricanes. It seemed as though the Lord had handpicked this lovely condo just for us, and our hearts were brimming with gratitude! As visitors came to see our new place, even they appreciated the beauty and felt the warmth of our sweet home.

About three weeks after we moved into our new condo, I went out to do some early morning errands while Dave was still sleeping. About thirty minutes into my errands, I heard the Lord clearly telling me to drive home immediately, even though I wasn't finished yet. I have learned over the years to always keep my ears turned upward towards heaven to hear His still small voice, so even though it didn't make sense, I obeyed. As I arrived at our condo, I was horrified to see water coming out the front door.

I rushed in and saw that the water heater was leaking. I woke up Dave and he turned off the water right away. Our landlords contacted a plumber, who showed us a huge crack in the water heater. He explained that it was about to burst, and if Dave hadn't turned off the water, it would have ruptured and damaged not only our entire condo, but also the condo below us. Dave and I were so appreciative of the Lord's steadfast protection, perfect timing, and divine intervention – and very grateful for how He led me to be obedient!

The following week, we received a call from our new landlords. They requested a meeting at their house as soon as we could arrange it. We had no idea what they wanted, or the reason for the urgency. Although we had an excellent rapport with our landlords, we really didn't know what to expect, so we prayed and also asked our friends to join us in prayer. We felt a peace as we drove to their home.

When we arrived, they warmly greeted us. As soon as

we sat down, Victor spoke with a strong Italian accent for emphasis, but the twinkle in his eyes belied his gruffness. He declared, "I am about to offer you a deal you cannot refuse." Dave and I looked at each other in astonishment, not knowing what to make of this unusual pronouncement.

But then our hearts plummeted as he went on to explain that even though they promised us we could rent long term, there had been a change in plans. They would be relocating to North Carolina to enjoy the mountains, cooler weather, and hiking. They decided they were going to sell all three of their condos in Florida and buy a house in North Carolina.

Our mouths must have dropped open in shock, so immediately Victor launched into the deal we could not refuse. He told us that they were aware of our financial situation and that we did not qualify for a mortgage. However, they really wanted to make it possible for us to purchase their condo. We were stunned when they offered to sell it to us and to finance our mortgage! They required only a small down payment and promised to cover most of the closing costs as well as pay any current assessments that were owed to the Condo Association.

We truly felt the divine intervention of our loving Heavenly Father in that room. The four of us prayed together, and Dave and I felt the Lord leading us to accept their extremely kind and generous offer. We could hardly wrap our minds around our Heavenly Father's breathtaking gift.

"For nothing will be impossible with God."
Luke 1:37 NASB

The settlement table can become very interesting when a professional boxer and a professional entertainer are seated at it. We laughed so hard as Victor imitated "Rocky" the boxer and Dave belted out a Frank Sinatra song. The lawyer said that he had never experienced such an unusual and entertaining settlement meeting!

When we shared this incredible story with friends and family, they were astonished to hear about this astounding blessing in our lives. After four years of financial struggles in Florida, we could hardly believe this gift that the Lord had placed in our hands. To this day we stand in awe and deep gratitude when we realize what a miraculous intervention our Heavenly Father orchestrated on our behalf!

"Now to Him who is able to do far more abundantly beyond all that we ask or think, according to the power that works within us, to Him be the glory in the church and in Christ Jesus to all generations, forever and ever. Amen." Ephesians 3:20-21 NASB

It was such a joyous season as Dave and I basked in the condo miracle, pinching ourselves to know that it was real. Our compassionate and gracious *Yeshua* had opened the door and provided all that was necessary. Our hearts were full with the goodness of the Lord.

"O taste and see that the LORD is good;
How blessed is the man who takes refuge in Him!"
  Psalm 34:8 NAS

The years that we have spent in Florida have proven to be life-giving and fruitful in so many ways. The time we spend with family is priceless, and we will be forever grateful that the Lord directed us to move to this earthly paradise. It has truly been a life of adventure lived with gratitude and trust one day at a time.

Dave and I are getting busier with our musical duo *The Winn Winn Situation,* and we cherish the opportunities to bring joy through music into the various facilities for the elderly in South Florida. And my work as Entertainment Director on *Cruising with the King* continues to fulfill my craving for adventure.

With the Lord's prompting, Dave and I felt led to begin a Wednesday evening fellowship with our dear friends Rick and Sherry. We wanted an opportunity to invite people who might not otherwise visit a congregation. Every week we meet in Rick and Sherry's home for dynamic worship and powerful prayer, and Rick delivers a very timely and anointed message. Dave and I are blessed to serve on the worship team. Since we began meeting together, we have welcomed many people from diverse religious backgrounds into our fellowship. Several people from the condo community have come to visit and have experienced the joy of the Lord! Our fellowship has grown, and we have a strong core group of people. We have bonded deeply and continually pray for each other as we navigate through some very challenging seasons of life.

New doors are opening for me at First Care, giving me an opportunity to counsel clients in the clinics who are considering abortion. It is important before making such a life changing decision that these women count the cost and learn about other options. Abortion is not the "quick easy fix" that many consider it to be. Abortion is a wound to the soul. I know this pain not only from my personal experience, but also from counseling hundreds of grieving post abortive women over the years. We at First Care want to make sure they know that there are other options available before making a decision that could affect them for the rest of their lives. No matter what decision the client makes, First Care offers compassionate care and will refer the client for abortion recovery if necessary.

I trust that the meaning of redemption has come alive

to you as you have read through the pages of this book. I am in awe as I behold how the Lord turned around so many of my challenging life events for His glory. My rainbow in the night shines brighter with each passing day, and He has opened my eyes to see that the rainbow was truly there all the time! My cup overflows with gratitude for all the many blessings my magnificent Lord *Yeshua* has poured into my life. I am eternally grateful to Him for His daily love and mercies.

> *"The LORD's lovingkindnesses indeed never cease,*
> *For His compassions never fail.*
> *They are new every morning;*
> *Great is Your faithfulness."*
>
> Lamentations 3:22-23 NASB

What the next season holds is known only to our wonderful Lord *Yeshua*. I continue trusting Him daily, with my heart open to what may unfold in the coming days. This passage from Matthew is my life Scripture, and I live it out one day at a time.

> *"For this reason I say to you, do not be worried about your life, as to what you will eat or what you will drink; nor for your body, as to what you will put on. Is not life more than food, and the body more than clothing? Look at the birds of the air, that they do not sow, nor reap nor gather into barns, and yet your heavenly Father feeds them. Are you not worth much more than they? And who of you by being worried can add a single hour to his life? And why are you worried about clothing? Observe how the lilies of the field grow; they do not toil nor do they spin, yet I say to you that not even Solomon in all his glory clothed himself like one of these. But if God*

187

so clothes the grass of the field, which is alive today and tomorrow is thrown into the furnace, will He not much more clothe you? You of little faith! Do not worry then, saying, "What will we eat?' or "What will we drink?' or "What will we wear for clothing?' For the Gentiles eagerly seek all these things; for your heavenly Father knows that you need all these things. But seek first His kingdom and His righteousness, and all these things will be added to you."

Matthew 6:25-33 NASB

I continue to remind myself that as I go through the process of sanctification, there will be plenty of challenges along the way. I am not perfect, but as I come to know *Yeshua* more and follow Him more closely, I am being shaped more into His image day by day.

"Therefore we do not lose heart. Though outwardly we are wasting away, yet inwardly we are being renewed day by day." II Corinthians 4:16

Spiritual growth is a process, not a onetime event.

Before I came to know *Yeshua* personally, I could not possibly imagine the healing, peace, joy, and freedom that I would find in Him. But when I chose to accept His death as payment for my sins, to make Him Lord and Savior of my life, and to invite Him into my heart, then I could truly say, *Ani khofshiya*! I am free!

If you have not yet made this life changing choice, I invite you to ask *Yeshua* into your heart right now. He offers unfathomable transformation and will fill you with hope, peace, purpose, and joy. If you would like to receive

Yeshua, pray this simple and heartfelt prayer with me:

Dear Yeshua,

Please forgive me for all my sins. I want You to be my Savior and the Lord of my life. I invite you into my heart right now. I am grateful that through your death, I can now enjoy eternity in heaven with you. Thank you for your precious sacrifice on my behalf. Amen.

If you have prayed this prayer, *nikadot*! You are now a child of God. Your sins are forgiven, *Yeshua* lives in your heart, and He has prepared a place for you in eternity with Him. I would love to hear from you! Please e-mail me at goldalah@icloud.com.

Thank you for joining me on my redemptive journey. My desire is that *Rainbow in the Night* has brought hope and encouragement to you. I hope and pray that your rainbow in the night gets brighter every day as you experience the unsurpassable love, grace, and peace of *Yeshua* the Messiah!

Resources

For help with unplanned pregnancy and abortion recovery:
- PalmBeachWC.org
- Care-Net.org
- HeartbeatInternational.org
- JustTheFacts.org
- AfterAbortion.org
- SurrenderingTheSecret.com
- HopeAfterAbortion.org
- MyAshesToBeauty.com

For 24/7 confidential help with unplanned pregnancy related issues:
- Option line: 1-800-712-HELP
  Online help: optionline.org
- After Abortion National Helpline: 1-866-482-5433
  Online help: nationalhelpline.org
- Suicide intervention/serious self-harm:
  1-800-273-8255

Bible studies and devotionals for abortion recovery available on Amazon:
- Cochrane, Linda. *Forgiven and Set Free.* Grand Rapids, MI: Baker Books, 1986, 1991, 1996, 2015.
- Layton, Pat. *Surrendering the Secret: Healing the Heartbreak of Abortion.* Nashville, TN: Lifeway Press, 2008, 2018. Video series also available.
- Woodley, Julie. *Into My Arms.* Grand Rapids, MI: Zondervan, 1973, 1978, 1984. Video series also available.
- Covert, Keven C. *Brick by Brick: Healing His Way, A Devotional and Journal for Healing a Woman's Heart.* Bloomington, IN: Westbow Press, 2015.

• *Restoring the Heart Ministries* has resources available for abortion recovery, sexual abuse recovery, and sexual trafficking recovery. RTHM.cc

Retreats and Workshops for Abortion Recovery:

• *Rachel's Vineyard*: 1-877-467-3463
www.rachelsvineyard.org
• *A Choice to Heal*: 1-860-267-6393
www.achoicetoheal.com

Books for Abortion Recovery:

• Burke, PhD., Theresa with Reardon, PhD., David C. *Forbidden Grief: The Unspoken Pain of Abortion.* Springfield, IL: Acorn Books, 2002, 2007.

• Stanford, Susan and Hazard, David. *Will I Cry Tomorrow? Healing Post Abortion Trauma.* Old Tappan, NJ: Fleming H. Revell Company, 1986.

• Hayford, Jack W. *I'll Hold You in Heaven: Healing and Hope for the Parent Who Has Lost a Child Through Miscarriage, Stillbirth, Abortion, or Early Infant Death.* Bloomington, MN: Chosen Books, 1986, 1990, 2003.

Books for Freedom and Healing from the Trials and Traumas of Life:

• Allender, Dan. *The Wounded Heart: Hope for Adult Victims of Childhood Sexual Abuse.* Colorado Springs, CO: NavPress, 1990.

• Anderson, Neil T. *Victory Over the Darkness.* Bloomington, MN: Bethany House Publishers, 2000, 2013.

• Li, M.D., Celeste. *Triumph Over Suffering, A Spiritual Guide to Conquering Adversity.* Jupiter, FL: Plum Tree Ministries, 2009, 2010, 2013.

• Li, M.D., Celeste. *Triumph of Surrender, A Walk of Intimacy with Jesus.* Jupiter, FL: Plum Tree Ministries, 2016.

• Welch, Edward T. *Shame Interrupted: How God Lifts the Pain of Worthlessness & Rejection.* Greensboro, NC: New Growth Press, 2012.

Acknowledgments

I began writing this book in the late 90's, and it has definitely been a process and not an event! It would take another book to thank everyone who played such an integral role in my life's journey and also all those who offered kindness, love, support, and prayer all throughout the process. At the top of the list I want to thank *Yeshua* my amazing Messiah and Lord, who radically changed my life when I completely surrendered my heart to Him in 1974. I have never looked back and I am deeply grateful every day for His gift of joy and His loving presence in every aspect of my life!

I am very blessed to have a loving, Godly, talented, funny, and patient husband who has been my very best friend and life partner since we first met in 1971. Dave has always supported and encouraged me in the process of writing, even when it meant I needed to spend several days away from him at my writing retreats!

There are two couples who have provided their very lovely and peaceful homes for these writing retreats. I am deeply grateful to David and Jean, who offered their beach home in Avalon, New Jersey when I first began writing this book. I would like to thank our dear friends Bruce and Renie who provided their guest house in Delray Beach, Florida for the final year of my writing.

There have been special angels along the way - Christina and Nancy - who blessed me beyond words, and I will forever be grateful for their extreme kindness and generosity.

My family has been amazing. My sister Esther helped with some editing and wrote the beautiful forward for this book. She has loved me well and I have coveted her prayers and support throughout my journey. I am very grateful for our very deep and loving friendship in the Lord.

My younger sister Cathy is one of my heroes. She was very courageous as a single mom to raise her lovely son Daniel, and is now a happy grandmother! She has always encouraged me to write my life story.

My parents are in heaven but they passed on to me many wonderful gifts, including our mutual love for music. They have always supported my career in the helping profession, and their passion for the mentally challenged inspired me to pursue a career as a social worker.

I am deeply grateful for Aunt Henri and Uncle Paul, who graciously allowed me to live with them during a very difficult time in my life. They offered unconditional love, which helped me to feel safe during my in-depth therapy. Uncle Paul is no longer with us, but Aunt Henri "adopted" us (Mom #2) since both Dave and I lost our moms many years ago. I am grateful for the wonderful years we have shared with Mom #2 (Aunt Henri) since we moved to Florida in 2011. Sadly, she passed away on August 29, 2019 at the age of 94. She left us all with a wonderful and loving family legacy to always stay close as a family. I miss her very much, as we enjoyed many sweet times together. But I am grateful she is at peace in her heavenly home and she will live on in my heart forever!

My cousin Ellen and her daughter Kelly are precious to me. They have loved me unconditionally and offered wonderful advice and support, especially since our move to Florida. We are so very close.

I have so many wonderful and close friends and family all over the country and in Israel. Each of you played a part in my healing journey and I am so very grateful. Thank you Nina Bear for your love and support when we lived in Minnesota. Thank you Dr. Rhona for your abiding and loving friendship all these years, and for your lovely endorsement of this book. We have certainly been there for each other through thick and thin! Thank you Bruce and Joan Boydell for your Godly mentoring, and for freely offering your wisdom, support, love, and insight along the journey. And thank you for endorsing my book, Joanie.

Rick and Sherry, we are so blessed that the Lord moved the four of us to Delray Beach and that you only live five minutes away from us! Our friendship was made in heaven and we are so grateful to worship with you every week. I am very thankful to you, Sherry, for your amazing artistic talent and the gorgeous painting for the book cover.

I love and appreciate all my First Care sisters who continually love and pray for me as I write. Last, but certainly not least, I am deeply indebted to Dr. Celeste Li and her husband John for taking on this project. The Lord handpicked them to edit and publish *Rainbow in the Night: A Journey of Redemption*. This was divine intervention and I am deeply grateful.

There are so many unnamed people to acknowledge, but you know who you are and I thank each and every one of you for playing a part in loving and praying for me on this wonderful journey called life! *L'Chaim!* My prayer is that many lives will be transformed as a result of the Lord's amazing redemption as told throughout the pages of this book *"...for such a time as this"* (Esther 4:14).

About the Author

Although some of her accomplishments may sound ordinary, Jane "Goldie" Winn is anything but ordinary. It is her reliance upon the Lord which sets her apart, as He has faithfully given her the tools of His love and wisdom in all that she has achieved.

In 1993, Jane received a Master's Degree from the Graduate School of Social Work at Bryn Mawr College, Pennsylvania. She worked in private practice as a therapist until 1997, when she assumed the position of Client Services Director at Amnion Crisis Pregnancy Center in the Philadelphia area.

Jane and her husband Dave, happily married since 1974, relocated to Delray Beach, Florida, in 2011. Jane took a position as the Abortion Recovery Director at First Care Women's Clinic in West Palm Beach, where she trained and led a team of Abortion Recovery Facilitators. This team is responsible for leading Bible studies in the local churches for post abortive women in need of healing. Currently, Jane serves as a Client Advocate in the clinics. Her role is to come alongside the Clinic Directors as a counselor of clients who are in the throes of making a decision about their unplanned pregnancies.

A published author who enjoys public speaking, Jane has spoken in a variety of venues throughout the country. Yet this particular book was not birthed out of her education or degrees, but out of her relationship with the Lord and her love for people. Her compassion for those in desperate circumstances has prompted her to unfold her very life across these pages.

Jane is available to share her story of redemption every place the Lord leads. Her greatest desire is to bring hope and encouragement wherever she goes.

JaneGoldieWinn.com

Made in the USA
Lexington, KY
09 December 2019

58353274R00131